Jimi Hendrix
THE BLUESMAN

BY DAVE RUBIN

Photos courtesy of EXPERIENCE HENDRIX, L.L.C.
Used by permission

ISBN 0-7935-6575-8

EXPERIENCE
HENDRIX

EXCLUSIVELY DISTRIBUTED BY

HAL•LEONARD®
CORPORATION
7777 W. BLUEMOUND RD. P.O. BOX 13819 MILWAUKEE, WI 53213

Visit Hal Leonard Online at
www.halleonard.com

Visit EXPERIENCE HENDRIX Online at
www.jimi-hendrix.com

Jimi Hendrix
THE BLUESMAN

4   Introduction

6   CATFISH BLUES

10   VOODOO CHILE

15   KILLING FLOOR

18   BORN UNDER A BAD SIGN

25   ONCE I HAD A WOMAN

30   COME ON (PART I)

34   JAM 292

40   HEAR MY TRAIN A COMIN' (GET MY HEART BACK TOGETHER)
      (ACOUSTIC VERSION FROM *BLUES*)

44   HEAR MY TRAIN A COMIN' (GET MY HEART BACK TOGETHER)
      (FROM *WOODSTOCK*)

49   RED HOUSE
      (FROM *SMASH HITS*)

54   RED HOUSE
      (FROM *WOODSTOCK*)

57   GYPSY EYES

60   IN FROM THE STORM

64   Guitar Notation Legend

Introduction

"Blues is a part of America. It means Elmore James and Howlin' Wolf and Robert Johnson.
It means Muddy Waters and Bo Diddley…
Everybody has some blues to offer. My main thing is the blues."

—Jimi Hendrix

Had he *only* played the blues, Jimi Hendrix would have secured an honored place in the history of music. But, of course, he did much more than that. Hendrix's grasp of technique and lyricism was a revelation to guitarists of all stripes. His fusing of funky R&B with hard rock, his imaginative and fiery lead work, his advanced use of effects like wah-wah and Octavia, "backwards" guitar and flanging, tremolo and feedback—even his otherworldly songwriting—all combined to virtually redefine the rock guitar vocabulary. Hendrix's studio work with the Experience and his legendary live performances—dousing a Strat with lighter fluid and sitting it on fire at the Monterey Pop Festival in 1967, for example—made him both a textbook source of inspiration for generations of musicians and a symbol of the entire '60s counterculture. Showmanship aside, however, the one source of inspiration, the form and the tradtion, to which Jimi Hendrix the musician always returned time and again was the blues. Indeed, when his life and music are examined from the point of view of the deep bluesman, rather than the shocking psychedelic rock star, the true nature of Hendrix's electric genius is revealed.

Born Johnny Allen Hendrix on November 27, 1942, Hendrix was renamed James Marshall by his father, James "Al" Hendrix, who received custody of his son following a divorce from his wife Lucille. Al was an amateur saxophonist and an enthusiastic music fan, and the jump blues of Louis Jordan, Roy Milton, and Big Joe Turner rocked the Hendrix household in the '40s. Later in the decade, music would ignite the fire in young Jimmy as well, in the form of Muddy Waters' hot-wired country blues and John Lee Hooker's scalding boogies. Al took notice his son's interest in music one day after discovering broom straws scattered out around the foot of Jimmy's bed. When questioned, Jimmy confessed to having been strumming the broom like it was a guitar. Al found him an old, one-string ukulele, for which Jimmy gladly exchanged the broom.

By 1958, Al had purchased Jimmy a five-dollar, secondhand acoustic guitar from one of his friends, and with it, Jimmy formed his first band, the Velvetones. But after a three-month stint, Jimmy left the group to pursue his own interests. The following summer, Al purchased Jimmy his first electric guitar, a Supro Ozark 1950S, which he used when he joined the Rocking Kings. The Supro Ozark also accompanied Jimmy when he moved out of his father's house and into the United States Army, 101st Airborne, in 1961.

While stationed at Fort Campbell, Kentucky, Jimmy formed the King Casuals with bassist Billy Cox. After being discharged due to an injury he received during a parachute jump, Jimmy then began working as a session guitarist under the name Jimmy James, backing such acts as Ike and Tina Turner, Sam Cooke, the Isley Brothers, and Little Richard. Gigging extensively with Little Richard in 1964, Hendrix became entangled in a contract dispute with the mercurial artist and left to form his own band, Jimmy James and the Blue Flames. Hendrix was still performing under the name Jimmy James when Animals' bassist Chas Chandler first heard him play in Greenwich Village nearly a year later.

Chandler's first move was to change Jimmy's name to "Jimi." His second was to transport Hendrix to London, where, backed by Mitch Mitchell on drums and Noel Redding on bass, the newly-formed Jimi Hendrix Experience quickly became the talk of the city. For their debut single, the Experience chose to cover L.A. band the Leaves' "Hey Joe." Almost immediately afterwards came the 1967 release of *Are You Experienced?*, their first full-length album, featuring songs like "Foxey Lady," "Fire," and, of course, the title track. It remains one of the most popular albums in all of rock history. For the first time in a studio recording, the extraordinary, bluesy rock guitar that Chas Chandler saw in its embryonic form in New York was brought to light.

While his early influences included the aforementioned Muddy Waters and John Lee Hooker—as well as B.B. King and the Delta slide slasher Elmore James—other electric heroes of Jimi's included Howlin' Wolf's two main string-mashers, Wild Willie Johnson and Hubert Sumlin. Jimi was always attracted to edgy, uninhibited guitarists. Shades of Johnson's distorted, jazzy forays, for example, color the extended live versions of "Red House." Legendary left-handed pickers like Albert King and Otis Rush likewise commanded Jimi's attention and curiosity, as he wondered about the snaky sound emanating from right-handed axes flipped upside down with restringing.

Besides raw country blues and soulful R&B, Jimi was obviously hip to the rock 'n' roll of Chuck Berry and the Woody Guthrie-inspired folk music of Bob Dylan. He was coming of age during the cultural revolution fomenting in the early '60s, which would create an environment of unparalleled musical experimentation in places as diverse as San Francisco and Liverpool. At the vanguard were electric guitarists, who mixed blues, rock 'n' roll, folk, and even classical music into a sensual and sense-altering style called "psychedelia." Jimi would take the primal expressiveness of the blues, the energy of '50s rock, the funk of R&B, and the poetic lyrics of Dylan, combine them with his own original approach, and channel it through the electronic potential of the electric guitar.

Two giants of American music, seemingly bipolar in style, perhaps throw Jimi's art into sharpest relief— Delta blues legend Robert Johnson and jazz saxophone virtuoso John Coltrane.

Some of the parallels between Johnson and Hendrix are almost uncanny—their careers were similar in length, and both guitarists died tragically at the age of 27. Both were also poised at the apex of their careers, through coincidence or otherwise, to funnel the accomplishments of their predecessors through their own immense artistic vision. The tendrils from Johnson's roots spread to the boogie patterns of John Temple, the single-note filigree of Lonnie Johnson and Scrapper Blackwell, and the driving slide guitar rhythms of Son House, to name only the most obvious. To be sure, there were others undergoing this musical epiphany—in the '30s for instance, Bukka White, like Johnson, was also streamlining and regulating country blues in the form of steadier rhythm and standardized chord changes—but it was Johnson, with his total command of the idiom, who would meld his considerable singing, songwriting, and spectacular guitar accompaniment abilities with his personal vision of demonic possession to help point the way to the electric ensembles that Muddy Waters would pioneer in Chicago some ten years later.

Coltrane, on the other hand, left a musical legacy of free-spirited improvisational genius that led to revolutionary, unstructured "free jazz" of the '60s. Much as Hendrix's music felt as though it could go anywhere he willed it and still make sense, Coltrane's work is marked by his own sense of freedom. Whether it was *Kind of Blue* with Miles Davis, the epochal *My Favorite Things,* the landmark *Giant Steps*, or even the posthumously released *Intersteller Space*, where his unaccompanied tenor blows over the drums of Rashied Ali, Coltrane's blues roots were indelibly printed on his sound. This latter album, with song titles like "Mars, Fourth from the Sun" and "Venus, Second from the Sun; Love," begs comparison to Jimi's "Third Stone from the Sun" from *Are You Experienced?* Most telling of all, though, is *Coltrane Plays the Blues*. Like Jimi's many epic concert versions of "Red House," Coltrane takes standard blues changes mostly in an unadorned twelve-bar format and runs the gamut of his personal blues history. Both Hendrix and Coltrane acknowledge the rich tradition of the form by quoting liberally from classic country and urban blues, R&B, and gospel music. Most significantly, both then move on to stretch the harmonic, melodic, and tonal boundries of their respective instruments. Unfettered improvisation had become the norm for contemporary jazz in the late '60s, but Jimi was the first to challenge the commonly-accepted precepts of blues soloing with his extended jams.

Though it was downplayed while he was alive, Jimi had a personal interest in jazz as a way to grow musically. The arranger Gil Evans even wanted to put him in an orchestral setting, as had been done with Charlie Parker. Alas, the record companies only wanted Jimi to continue cranking out more Foxey Lady's, and then he was gone before he could realize his dreams. One posthumous album, *Nine to the Universe*, contains a selection of relaxed fusion jams with Billy Cox and Dave Holland (bass), Mitch Mitchell and Buddy Miles (drums), Jim McCartey and Larry Lee (guitars), and jazz organist Larry Young (from John McLaughlin's band). Hearing Jimi in this context gives us a brief but tantalizing hint at where he could have been headed. Likewise, "South Saturn Delta," recorded at a studio jam with the Brecker Brothers in 1969, also shows Jimi's flowering jazz inclinations. The fact that he talked about studying music and learning to read further attests to the seriousness of his intentions.

Inasmuch as he did not get to more fully delve into jazz, Jimi did, of course, bring his full creative impulses to bear on his blues. Here he was totally at home with the language and structures of the art form. No doubt he felt as John Coltrane did: that the blues were so endemic to his musical sensibility—he was so comfortable in their secure cycle of chord changes—he could indulge his imagination to its greatest extent. The thirteen lucky numbers chosen for this collection range from the acoustic country blues of "Hear My Train A Comin'" (12-string version) to the hypnotic funk blues of "Gypsy Eyes." Of course, the essential "Red House" is here in two incarnations as well. It would be a mistake, however, to believe that Jimi's blues begin and end with this twelve-bar anthem. His reach matched his grasp, so that he could turn Wolf's classic "Killing Floor" into a flag-waving rave-up of outlandish proportions, or, in a different vein, take the country grid of John Lee Hooker and Muddy Waters and transmute them into his monumental "Voodoo Chile" and "Voodoo Child (Slight Return)."

So look on yonder's wall, get your walking cane handed down, and let us drive south with Jimi, into the land of the blues...

Catfish Blues
(:Blues)

The main guitar theme of this version of the Delta standard was probably heard by Jimi in Muddy Waters's "Rolling Stone" (1950) or "Still a Fool" (1951). He may also have been aware of John Lee Hooker's "Catfish" from 1951, with a different instrumental accompaniment. Besides being the basis for "Voodoo Chile," this modal opus of Delta blues gave Jimi an excuse, especially in concert, to run wild through his blues roots and beyond.

FIGURE 1

Study

In the protean blues key of E, this riff is one of the "big daddies." Using the open position of the E blues scale, the defining notes (root, ♭3rd, ♭5th, and ♭7th) are all touched upon in a bold statement. The ♭3rd (G) is bent one quarter step, as a pickup on beat 4 of the preceding measure, resolving to the root (E) and major 3rd (G♯) on beat 1 of this one-measure phrase. Continuing with the fundamental blues concept of tension and release, Jimi then bends the 4th (A) one half step to the ♭5th (B♭) before releasing and resolving again to the root. On beat 4, the process is repeated. Note Jimi's personal contribution to the language of the blues with a semi-harmonic between beats 2 and 3. Even when playing a lowdown country blues, he heard heavenly choruses in his head!

Performance

Play the bend on the low E string by pulling down with your middle finger, then move quickly to the E note on the second fret of the D string while simultaneously hammering from G to G♯ on string 3 with your index finger. To execute the next lick, pluck the high, open E string with your right hand middle finger while using the pick to strike the A note on string 3. I suggest using the left hand middle finger to push up the bend.

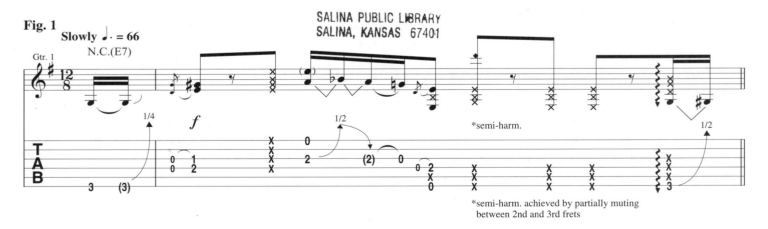

*semi-harm. achieved by partially muting
between 2nd and 3rd frets

FIGURE 2

Study

This jaunty phrase is lifted almost whole from Muddy Waters's "Still a Fool" (with blues harp virtuoso Little Walter on second guitar). The bending of the 4th (A) to the ♭5th (B♭), is one of the oldest and most basic blues guitar licks. With the release to the ♭3rd (G) and resolution to the root (E), a short but complete blues thought is expressed.

Performance

In order to keep the logical fingering system begun in Figure 1, use your ring finger for the D (♭7th) note on the third fret of the second string. This way you can still comfortably employ your middle finger for the G-string bends.

Fig. 2

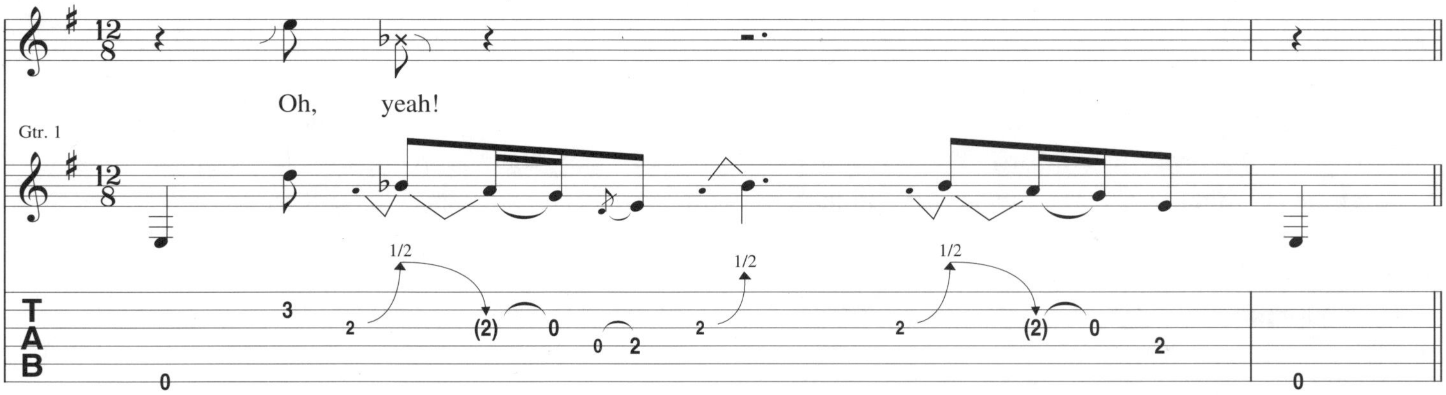

FIGURE 3

Study

Again taking his cue from "Still a Fool" (and perhaps from other sources as well), Jimi doubles his vocal melody with his guitar. Rather than playing in the same octave as his voice, however, he opts for the octave *below*. The effect is extremely powerful and menacing.

The outstanding artist always does the unexpected, and Jimi was no exception. He does not follow each sung syllable with its equivalent note and rhythm, but instead intuitively embellishes and alters pitches. After punctuating the word "Lord" with a sassy double stop (C/G), for the word "on" (sung melismatically B to D) he plays C♯ to E, a 2nd above the melody. Likewise, at the end of his unison passage, where he sings "step" (A to G), he plays A to G to E, for musical resolution.

Performance

Starting with your ring finger on the B notes at the seventh fret (string 6) and your index finger on the D note at the fifth fret (string 5), use a combination of those two digits to play the entire phrase. The bend for "Lord" should be accomplished with the index finger, and the ones for "front" with the ring finger.

Fig. 3

an' I   sat   down, Lord, —   on — her —   front —   step. —

*played behind the beat

FIGURE 4

Study

Jimi starts his solo with a first inversion triad (E/G#) and its companion, an E dominant triple stop (B, D, G#—or 5th, ♭7th, 3rd). These chord forms probably have their antecedents in open-tuned slide guitar (particularly D and E) and usher in his solo with a roar. They are especially effective when played in a trio context, because they can function as both rhythm and lead.

Performance

Barre across the top three strings with your index finger, placing your middle finger on the G string (thirteenth fret) for the E/G# triad. Play the E7 triple stop as if you were forming an open position D7 chord.

Rhythmically, these three measures are a bear to duplicate. Alternate down and up strokes the way mandolin (and jazz) players pick. Go for feel, rather than outright mimicry, and you will succeed in conveying the burst of energy so necessary to this section.

Fig. 4
Guitar Solo

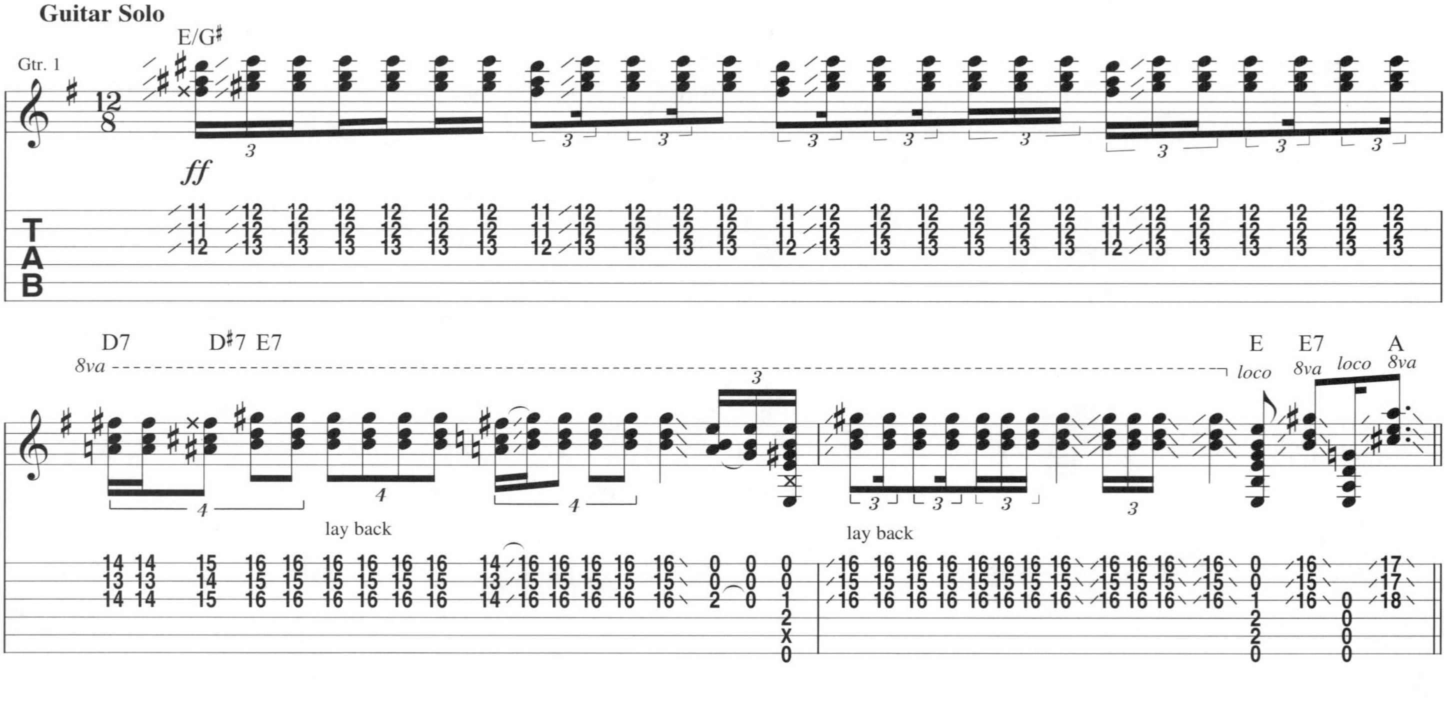

FIGURE 5

Study

After Mitch's drum solo, Jimi wah-wahs his way back in, and the band dynamically drops to a whisper. Jimi free associates for a while, noodling with the wah and whammy bar, before signaling a tempo and theme change as an outro. He starts with the hook from "Cat's Squirrel," which had recently been covered by Cream on their debut album, *Fresh Cream* (1967).

Performance

By fingering the E chord in the standard "folk guitar" manner (index finger on string 3, middle finger on string 4), you can easily snap the A/E chord with your middle finger (string 4), ring finger (string 3), and pinkie finger (string 2). Use your middle finger to bend the third string up.

Fig. 5
Outro Solo

FIGURE 6

Study

In what could be seen as another nod towards his compatriot, Eric Clapton, Jimi ends his outro solo with a one-measure quote from "Spoonful." With a combination of double stops (B/G), single notes (E and G), and a whomping open chord (E), he suggests harmonic movement from E to G to E.

Performance

Use your middle finger (string 6) and index finger (string 5) to grab the G dyads. The rest is elementary, my dear Watson.

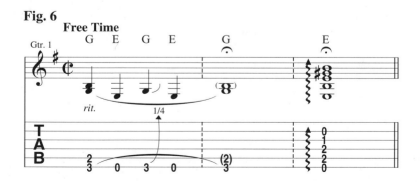

Fig. 6
Free Time

Voodoo Chile
(Electric Ladyland)

This autobiographical fantasy based on "Catfish Blues" is a testament to Jimi's primary blues sources. Though more restrained than the live versions, the classic studio track is, nonetheless, replete with whistling feedback and whammy bar whimsy—heady stuff to pull on the blues in 1968! And, where "Catfish Blues" was merely the modest story of a randy bluesman, "Voodoo Chile" aspires to be nothing less than the mythical legend of Jimi's life.

With superior sidemen like organist Steve Winwood and bassist Jack Cassady (from the Jefferson Airplane), along with the redoubtable Mitch Mitchell on "tubs," Jimi was free to play more single-note lead than on the trio's concert versions. Listen closely, and you can almost feel Muddy, Hooker, Lightnin', and B.B. peering over his shoulder as he works over his Strat.

FIGURE 1

Study

The pickup and first two measures contain some muscular open E position licks that immediately set the stage for the fifteen-minute blues concerto that follows.

Performance

This is pretty basic stuff, right out of the Lightnin' Hopkins or John Lee Hooker school of E blues guitar riffs, but Jimi's fluidity and supple phrasing add an aura of sensuality absent in the music of his mentors.

Try the trill with your middle finger. In measure 1, assign your middle finger to the notes that occur at the second fret, and your ring finger to the note at the third fret. Then, use your ring finger to slide from the second fret to the fourth fret on string 3, nailing the D note on string 2 at the third fret with your middle finger.

Fig. 1

Tune Down 1 Step:

① = D   ④ = C
② = A   ⑤ = G
③ = F   ⑥ = D

FIGURE 2

Study

Jimi interrupts his instrumental intro to sing along with his guitar, "Well…I'm a voodoo child… Lord, I'm a voodoo child." Similar to Figure 3 of "Catfish Blues," Jimi doubles his vocal line with his ax. Where he previously played an octave below his voice, here he floats an octave *above* for an otherworldly, celestial effect.

Using the basic minor pentatonic blues scale, Jimi follows the melody of his vocal line closely. The exceptions are the word "child" in both measures, where he melismatically sings three notes over one syllable. In measure 1, he incorporates the released D note as an embellishment between the bent E and pulled-off B.

In measure 2, he alters two pitches, pitting the played A against the sung G, and the played G against the sung E. It is possible that this was accidental and that his intention was to be in sync, as "happy accidents" occur regularly in the hands of the masters. The result is a bit of ear-tickling harmony in the midst of a phrase that resolves to the tonic E (vocally and instrumentally) anyway.

Performance

If you start with your index finger on the B note at the twelfth fret, you can use the standard blues scale fingerings without shifting your hand position. Pay close attention to those 1 1/4 step bends in measure 1 for that vibrant blues *edge!*

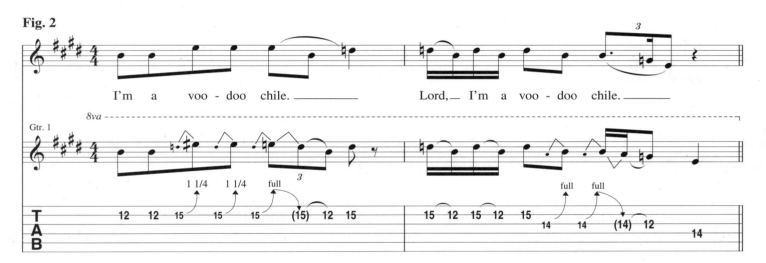

Fig. 2

FIGURE 3

Study

After Jimi's first chorus, a dramatic chordal climb from C to D to E, he takes a brief four-measure solo as an interlude. The middle two measures have a series of Buddy Guy-inspired bends and releases. To modern ears brought up on whammy bar manipulation, it almost sounds like a sequence of dive bombs. In reality, it is Jimi's superb string handling that produces the feeling of an "out of body" experience.

Theoretically, this is something less than quantum physics. In the simplest terms, the 4th (A) is bent and released either a full step to the 5th (B) or one half step to the ♭5th, in rapid succession. Against the modal E vamp of the rhythm, this musical rollercoaster is at once exhilarating and dizzying!

Performance

Lock your ring finger on the fourteenth fret of string 3, back it up with the middle and index fingers, and let 'er rip.

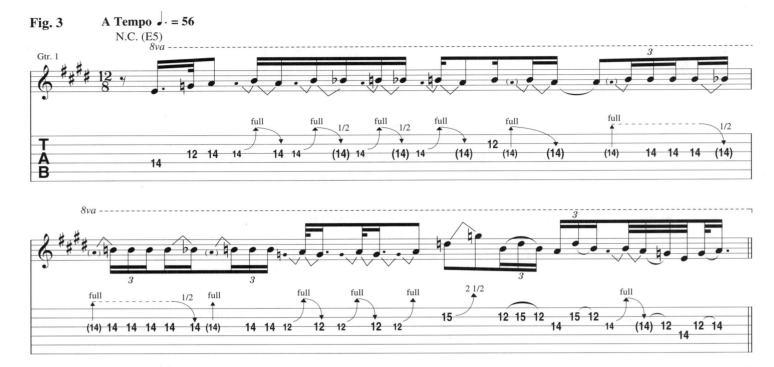

Fig. 3   A Tempo ♩. = 56

FIGURE 4

Study

Using the chorus as a springboard once again, Jimi launches himself skyward with a pyrotechnic display of fretboard fireworks. This four-measure excerpt has, besides copious sixteenth and thirty-second notes, a number of wide interval bends à la Monsieur Guy. The resulting screams and howls conjure images of secret tribal ceremonies and unleashed passions.

Notice that just prior to this figure Jimi begins his furious assault with a two-step bend of G (♭3rd) to B (5th). At the end of measure 1, he adds the D (♭7th) below the G and bends the double stop two whole steps to B/F♯ (5th/9th)!

In measure 3, Jimi *overbends* two and one-half steps; on beat 1 he tortures his B string by pushing the D (♭7th) up to G (10th!), and on beat 3 he tests the mettle of his G string by forcing the pitch from A (4th) to D.

The entire four-measure passage is framed neatly and tied together thematically when Jimi repeats the bend of G to B on the last two beats of measure 4.

Performance

The single notes at the fifteenth fret should be bent with the pinkie (yes, the pinkie), backed up by the ring, middle, and index fingers. The double-stop bend at the end of measure one requires the pinkie finger (E string) and ring finger (B string).

The G-string bend at the fourteenth fret in measure 2 can be stretched with the ring finger, backed up by the middle and index fingers.

Fig. 4

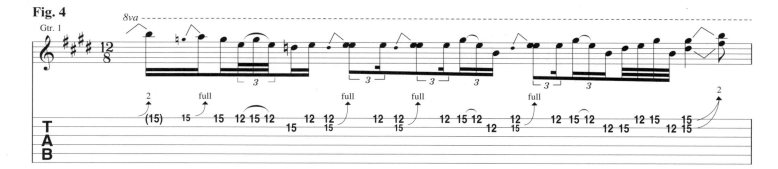

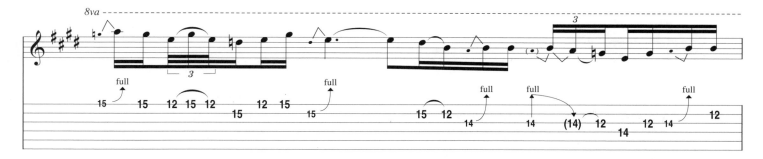

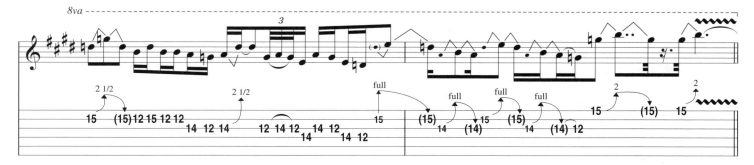

FIGURE 5

Study

Taking a page from the blues guitar method of the great Albert Collins (who replaced Jimi in Little Richard's band in 1965), Jimi trills at three times the speed of the "Master of the Telecaster" for four measures. He selects the 5th (B) and ♭7th (D) notes for his trill, providing a consonant blues harmony against the modal E drone.

Repetition is an excellent device for creating musical tension, as amply demonstrated here by Jimi. He begins to release the tension, in dramatic fashion, when he gradually depresses the whammy bar on his Strat. Climaxing the image of a long, slow descent, Jimi jumps down to the open position E blues scale, returning to the country blues licks from whence he sprung.

Performance

Anchor your index finger at the twelfth fret and hammer your pinkie up and down for all you're worth. Oh yeah—pick the B string *once,* using the force of your trill to keep the string excited for the duration of the phrase.

Fig. 5

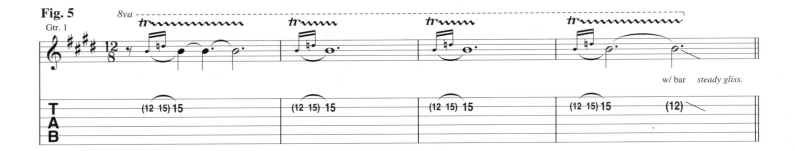

FIGURE 6

Study

Near the end of Mitch Mitchell's drum solo, Jimi reaches way beyond traditional blues. Sounding like nothing less than an electrified snake charmer, he veers into the E Mixolydian (dominant) mode, playing entirely on the G string. The timbre and legato phrasing of this section definitely puts one in mind of John Coltrane's soprano sax excursions on tunes like "My Favorite Things" (*My Favorite Things*, 1960).

Performance

These two measures should be played with one finger by sliding up and down the G string. The decision is yours, but the index finger would seem to be the logical choice.

The tremolo picking in measure 2 requires steady and equal force applied to the down and up pick strokes. Be sure to pick from your elbow and forearm, more than from your wrist. It is the secret of fast bluegrass flatpicking.

Though Chuck Berry is probably the initial source, Jimi phrases these double stops like a whirling dervish. In fact, with the drum pattern underneath, the cadence is also reminiscent of a bolero, offering further proof of his eclecticism and innovative experimentation.

Fig. 6

Killing Floor
(Radio One)

Though it is known that Jimi Hendrix met Howlin' Wolf and even sat in with his band, it is not documented what Wolf thought of this version of his 1965 classic—or if he even heard it. Hubert Sumlin reports that Wolf loved Hendrix (even offering him Hubert's spot in the band!), but this howling blues-rocker may have given him pause. That said, this rendition kicks serious booty! Similar to the slashing version that blew a generation of folkies clean out of their seats at Monterey, it is a technical challenge to play it at Jimi's tempo. Note that after his unaccompanied intro, the bass line becomes one that Buddy Guy used in "I've Got My Eye on You," as well as other tunes.

FIGURE 1

Study

The six-measure intro fairly screams, "Look out!" as it bulls its way towards resolution. The first four measures are based on an A minor pentatonic vamp using the root (A), ♭7th (G), and ♭3rd (C). Included are two "West Side of Chicago" double stops (D/A and C/G) as harmonic ballast. Additionally, Jimi sneaks in G/E♭ in measure 3, and G/D in measure 4. Both add a dash of blues scale harmony within the rather tight confines of the vamp.

Even a cursory listen to Wolf's version will show that Jimi's intro to this point bears little resemblance. In measure 5 though, he inserts the A bass line similar to the one that drives the original—the only difference being the use of the gritty ♭3rd (C) after the root (A), as opposed to the major 3rd (C♯). Measure 6 then resolves to the V7 chord (E7) as per the Howlin' Wolf recording.

Performance

As notated under the staff, attach your hand at the fifth fret by hooking your thumb over the low E string. The quarter-step bends at the eighth fret in measures 1 and 2 should be yanked down by the pinkie finger.

A loose and aggressive approach is required to achieve the necessary level of controlled chaos in this passage. The down-and-up motion of the pick hand should originate from the elbow, as well as the wrist.

Fig. 1
Intro
Fast Blues Rock ♩ = 156

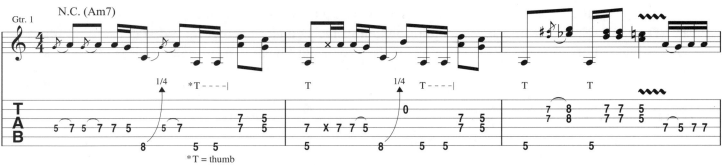

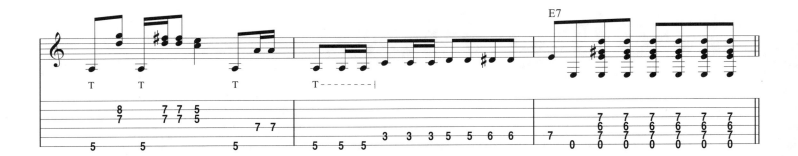

FIGURE 2

Study

Quoting from the head of the original, Jimi manufactures the first twelve measures of his solo around intervals of a 6th. In Figure 2, he enlists C#/E and B/D, resolving to an inverted A major triad (A/C#). In his inimitable way, Jimi seamlessly adds in the recurring bass line after the chord, suggesting two independent guitar parts.

Performance

Use your middle finger on the G string and your ring finger on the high E for the double stops. Barre the fifth fret across the top three strings with your index finger for the triad, playing the hammer-on (C to C#) with your middle finger.

FIGURE 3

Study

Jimi takes the sequence from Figure 2 and moves it up the neck in a parallel manner to elucidate the IV (D) chord. Note that he indicates the resolution to the D major chord with a double stop in 3rds (A/F#), instead of the major triad. The effect is the same as in Figure 2, as he again splices in the bass line.

Performance

Follow the same fingering as in Figure 2.

Fig. 3

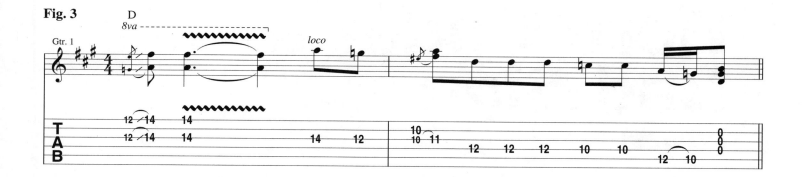

FIGURE 4

Study

One of the most important axioms in music, particularly blues, is that context is critical. Figure 4 is a perfect example, as the 6ths used to identify the V7 (E7) chord are exactly the same as those used in Figure 2 to identify the A chord. Because the bass is playing an E blues scale, the root of the chord change is clearly E (V). In this context, C#/E and B/D now become the 6th/root and 5th/♭7th of E.

The relationships over the IV (D) chord are the same.

Performance

Follow the same fingering as in Figures 2 and 3.

Fig. 4

Born Under a Bad Sign
(:Blues)

Like Eric Clapton and Stevie Ray Vaughan after him, Jimi Hendrix was profoundly influenced by the sinewy lead guitar style of Albert King. The wide interval bends, singing, vibratoed sustain, and dramatic phrasing—more controlled than that practiced by Buddy Guy—are evident in all of Jimi's blues. *Live Wire, Blues Power,* Albert's justly famous live album, was cut in 1967 at a Fillmore West concert where Jimi and John Mayall rounded out the bill. The older bluesman often imparted fatherly advice to Jimi when the two were together; it was a role that King fulfilled for Stevie Ray as well.

The original Albert King version of "Born Under a Bad Sign" has a quirky arrangement with three verses of varying length. Jimi plays just two twelve measure verses, maintaining the I chord for eight measures before moving to the V chord. For the remainder of the instrumental hoedown, the I chord is vamped like one long coda.

Though he is most likely playing a Strat, Jimi's unadorned trebly tone is remarkably reminiscent of Albert's Gibson Flying V guitar sound—mind over matter, or blues metaphysics?

FIGURE 1

Study

Though his take on "Born Under a Bad Sign" is an obvious homage to the "Velvet Bulldozer," Jimi was clearly searching with his own muse. As if to underscore this, he jumps outside of the tradition immediately after stating the main theme in the first twelve measures. The one-measure phrase of Figure 1 starts on the 9th (C♯), followed by the 4th (E), ♭3rd (D), root (B), and the root bent up one full step to the 9th—hardly your average, minor pentatonic blues lick. For those faint of heart, however, he completes the measure with a quick and friendly root (B) and 5th (F♯).

Performance

Play the C♯ with your ring finger, the E with your middle finger, the D with your index finger, and the bend with your ring or pinkie finger. The root and 5th can easily be snared with your index finger barring the top two strings at the seventh fret.

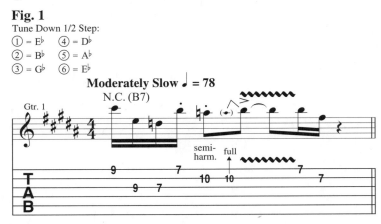

Fig. 1

FIGURE 2

Study

Following his irreverent opening, Jimi proceeds to demonstrate his knowledge of the "Albert King String Bending System," bending the ♭7th (A) to the root (B), then the 4th (E) to the 5th (F♯), before resolving to the root.

In measure 2 of this three-measure fragment, Jimi bends the 4th (E) one half step to the ♭5th (F) before piggybacking another bend on top of that, to reach the 5th (F♯). Again he releases and resolves to the root. On beats 3 and 4 of the measure, Jimi pulls a real Albert out of his headband by bending the ♭3rd (D) a full step to the 4th (E). He then follows up in measure 3 by bending the 4th up a full step to the 5th (F♯) before dropping back and peeling off a super cool double-string bend.

Performance

Generally speaking, when in the root position of the blues scale, bends on the B string should be accomplished with the pinkie (backed up by the other fingers). Bends on the G string normally require the ring finger, with the ♭3rd being the exception. For a true taste of the Albert King vibe, *pull down* on this note with your index finger.

Now this double-string bend is a horse of a different color. Inasmuch as the B-string bend is a by-product of the G string bend, pull down on both strings with your index finger by making a small barre. The physical distance between strings should naturally allow for the upper string to rise approximately one half step more than the lower.

Fig. 2

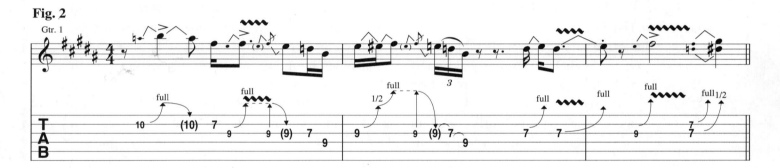

FIGURE 3

Study

Figure 3 begins the I chord vamp that Jimi blows hot and cool over until the fade-out. As a way of making the transition, he sculpts a one-measure double-stop and triple-stop phrase from the B blues scale and repeats it like a mantra for the next eight measures.

The basis for this pattern is one of the classic licks in blues history. The major 3rd (D♯) is hammered on from the ♭3rd (D), followed by a triple stop (B, E, G♯) that could be interpreted as an E/B major triad (IV chord). Jimi adds his own embellishment on top of this "cliché" by hammering three triple stops out of the blues box. The overall effect of this one-measure motif is of a I-IV chord change.

Performance

Use the index finger as an anchor at the seventh fret throughout this passage. Hammer the major 3rd with your middle finger, and use your index, middle, and ring fingers as barres to play the triple stop on beat 4.

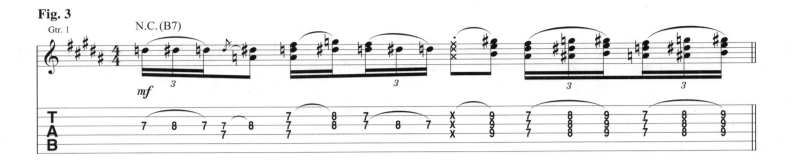

Fig. 3

FIGURE 4

Study

L.A. studio ace Larry Carlton once said that he felt Hendrix had taken the minor pentatonic scale as far as it could go. Whether that statement is true is certainly open for debate. What is undeniable, though, is that Jimi was exceptionally creative and fluent with those five notes.

Figure 4 highlights this beautifully. By making wider interval leaps, he firmly emphasizes the ♭3rd (D) and root (B) from the B blues scale. By quickly jumping between octaves, he adds dynamic interest to a scale that can easily sound predictable. The step up from the ♭3rd on the G string at the seventh fret to the root on the high E string bespeaks fundamental blues harmony, while on the second beat in measure 2, the breathless intervallic gambol from the ♭3rd *down* an octave to the low E string (bent up one half step) sounds like something a honking, R&B tenor saxman might rasp out. Jimi then follows up with a tight and fast series of pull-offs containing the 5th, 4th, ♭3rd, and root. On beat 4, he finesses a B.B.-esque harmony bend of the 4th to the 5th, held against the ♭7th, as entree into the next musical thought.

Performance

Standard root position blues scale fingerings will carry the day in this example. For the ♭3rd-to-root move on the second beat of measure 1, however, try using your middle finger for the root. The half step bend on the low E string should be accomplished by whomping down with the pinkie.

The ergonomically correct approach to the double-stop bend would be to place the ring finger on string 3 and the pinkie on string 2.

Fig. 4

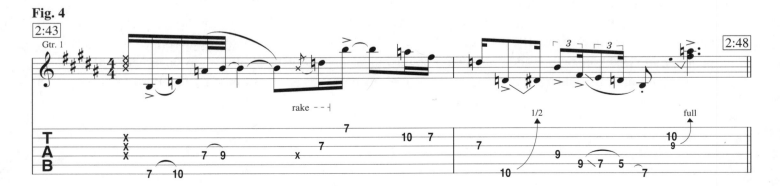

FIGURE 5

Study

This hypnotic interlude shows how Jimi could adapt a long, sustained modal jazz line for a blues context. With controlled feedback easily obtainable from his fingertips, he spins a hallucinatory, serpentine passage.

Taking advantage of the major/minor ambiguity of the bass line, Jimi casually slips in the 2nd (C#) and 6th (G#) degrees of the major scale. When combined with the basic blues scale, a Dorian mode (root, 2nd, ♭3rd, 4th, 5th, 6th, and ♭7th) is crafted, adding a melodic element to the gapped pentatonic scale. By keeping almost all the notes on the G string, Jimi is able to hammer, pull, and slide with very little pick attack.

Performance

You should be able to play this entire example with your index and ring fingers. Use your index finger for the notes at the seventh and eleventh frets and all glisses. The ring finger will nab the notes at the ninth and fourteenth frets.

Fig. 5

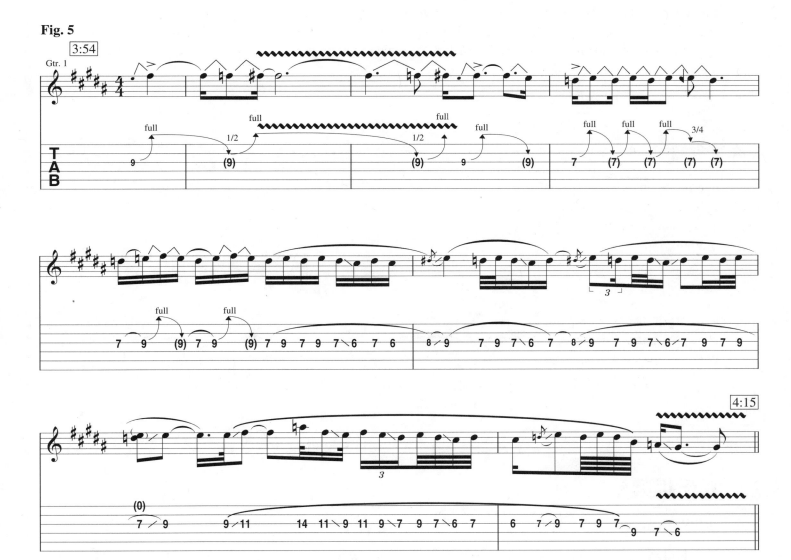

FIGURE 6

Study

Dipping his extra large hands into the jazzman's improvisational bag again, Jimi comes up weaving majestic-sounding octaves alongside a bravura string-sliding workout. Measure 1 contains the ♭7th and 2nd in "glissando-ing" octaves. Measure 2 has an incredible combination of glissed notes on beats 1 and 2 before it hits the ♭3rd, 4th, ♭5th, 5th, and ♭7th notes as a pickup into measure 3. Dig the octave A♯, at the imaginary twenty-fourth fret, that Jimi zooms up to in his unbridled enthusiasm!

In measure 4, Jimi shifts strings to play the ♭3rd, 5th, and 4th in octaves before reaching back into the B blues scale to begin his next foray.

Performance

Since the actual fretboard intervals between strings 4 and 2, as well as strings 3 and 1, are the same, use your index finger and pinkie for all octaves.

You can be sure that the amazingly smooth gliss in measure 2 does not have its roots in the classic blues tradition. (Fast Freddie King, though, does play a vaguely related bass string lick in the turnaround of the fourth chorus of "Hideaway.") Jimi's string control throughout the gliss is extraordinary, even by his high standards. Listen closely to this section, as the notation does not quite convey the steadiness of the ascending line on the low E string. It is so precise that one would be tempted to say that it was achieved with the whammy bar, instead of Jimi's magic index finger!

Fig. 6

*Past fretboard

FIGURE 7

Study

Following the octaves with a section of *sturm und drang*, Jimi chills out for eight measures. Then, after collecting his thoughts, he assumes the blues mantle once again and heads off in a new direction. This is a kinder and gentler Jimi, caressing and squeezing the strings at a lower volume and with more introspection. The three measures of Figure 7 are particularly lyrical.

Planting himself firmly in the root position of the B blues scale at the seventh fret, Jimi milks fluid bends out of the G string. In measure 1, he pushes the 4th to the 5th, frets the 5th on the B string, then re-bends the 4th a full step again. Holding the G-string bend over to measure 2, he performs a quick release back down to the 4th, followed by a snappy full-step bend of the ♭3rd up to the 4th. In the wink of an eye, he stops the bend at its apex and fingers the 4th unbent at the ninth fret. The result is a loopy, elastic series of swoops that tickles the ear as it engages the imagination. He closes out the measure with the ♭3rd (D) vibratoed, bent a quarter step, and resolved (at last!) to the root.

In measure 3, he starts a run down to the root on the low E string by bending the ♭7th one half step to the major 7th (!). The sixteenth-note passage of which it is a part obscures the full impact of this decidedly non-blues tone. In the softer, more melodic context of this section of his solo, however, it carries weight beyond its actual time value. Do not miss the inclusion of the very bluesy ♭5th (F) in this phrase—Jimi likes to cover all the bases when he can.

Performance

Bend the 4th (E) with your ring finger (backed up by the middle and index). The full-step bend of the ♭3rd to the 4th on beat 2 of the second measure should be executed with a mighty pull of the index finger.

Pull off from the ♭5th to the 4th, in the third measure, using your middle and ring fingers.

Fig. 7

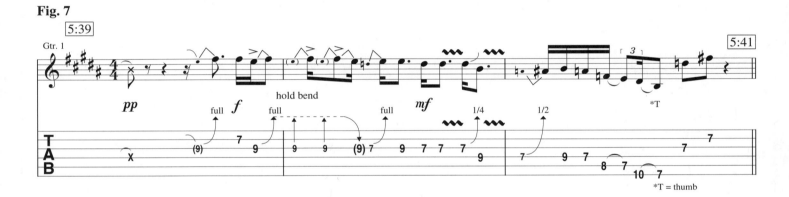

FIGURE 8

Study

Something to be aware of as you listen and play through "Born Under a Bad Sign" is Jimi's innate sense of composition. Even though, for all practical purposes, this is a one-chord instrumental groove, he still approaches it as a complete work with a beginning, end, and several discreet sections in between. Adding to the structure is the repetition of theme and motif.

Figure 8 is a variation on Figure 3. Though it is only two measures long, as opposed to the eight-measure increment of the former example, it serves the same function; as a dynamic interlude to set up the intense riffing that follows.

The main difference between the two examples is that the major 3rd (D♯) is not hammered onto within the double-stop sequence. Instead, Jimi employs only 4ths at the seventh and ninth frets.

Performance

After vibratoing the ♭3rd (D) with your index finger, set up the pull-off by placing your index finger on the D string at the seventh fret and your ring finger on the A string at the ninth fret.

The rest of the double stops and single notes can be accessed by playing the notes at the seventh fret with your index finger and the notes at the ninth fret with your ring finger.

Fig. 8

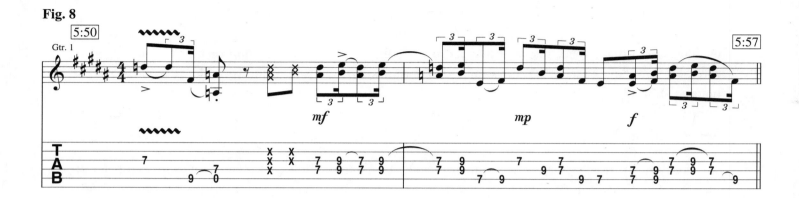

Once I Had a Woman
(:Blues)

Jimi's super-articulated string bending and whammy-bar antics gave his music a distinct "liquid time" feel. In "Once I Had a Woman" he achieves a similar effect through extreme dynamics of tempo between the very slow 12/8 time of the vocal section and the rampant, triple time of the solo. Within both sections, of course, there are many shades and nuances of phrasing.

This studio track was recorded with bassist Billy Cox and drummer Buddy Miles from the Band of Gypsies. Jimi's comfort level with this rhythm section was such that he could "stretch" (in all its meanings) beyond even *his* expanded boundaries.

Before we get into specific examples from "Once I Had a Woman," it would be useful to run down the chord progressions of the intro, verses, and solo. The key in the intro and verse is F♯ major.

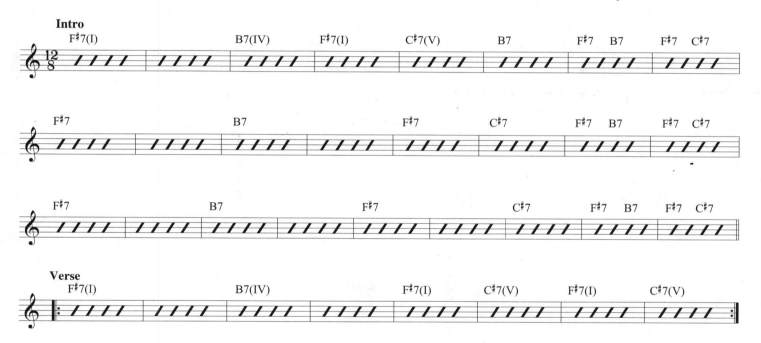

The solo is played in the key of E, over a one-chord vamp of E7♯9.

The intro and verses are similar in structure to "Sitting on Top of the World," a nine-measure blues, by the Mississippi Sheiks (1930). Notice that the third section of the intro is also nine measures in length. This subtle lengthening, shortening, and rearranging of chords was an accepted modus operandi of solo country blues guitarists of the pre-war era, but it is unusual to find it in "modern" ensemble blues.

FIGURE 1

Study

The extremely slow tempo (♩=30) of the intro and verses leaves plenty of opportunity for cramming thirty-second notes into every crevice. And make no mistake, Jimi takes advantage of the situation. In the third measure (over the IV chord) of the intro, through, he strolls leisurely on the D and G strings, in the root position of the F♯ blues scale.

After hammering and vibratoing the root of the chord (B), he cajoles the ♭7th (A) and 5th (F♯). The next two beats are then filled with a slinky series of G-string bends. First, the root is bent a full step to the 2nd (C♯). The ♭7th is pushed up to the root and then one and three quarter (!) steps to a quarter step shy of C♯. A release back to the ♭7th is followed by another full step bend. Then the 5th (F♯) and 4th (E) notes exit into the next measure.

Performance

The big bends are our main interest here. Shove the B note up with your ring finger and then muscle the A note by pulling down with your index finger. This requires some real "finger grease" in the lower fret positions, where the nut offers so much resistance.

Fig. 1

FIGURE 2

Study

Using the same improvisational tools (the F♯ blues scale with a selection of microtonal and wide interval bends) as in the previous six measures, Jimi outlines the I–IV–I–V (F♯–B–F♯–C♯) changes of the turnaround in measure 7 and 8.

The first and second beats of measure 1 emphasize the root (F♯), ♭7th (E), and ♭3rd (A). The bend of B one half step to C and one full step to C♯ creates a tension that resolves back to the sustained and vibratoed B (root of IV chord) on beat 3. Beat 4 also resolves to the root (B) of the change, after a full step bend to the 2nd (C♯).

In the second measure, Jimi leads in with the major 3rd (A♯) bent from the ♭3rd, before sustaining the ♭3rd (A) against the chord change. Our ears accept that dissonant *minor*-sounding ♭3rd after the major 3rd identifies the chord (F♯) as major. On the third beat Jimi sustains the C♯ (root of V chord) and then bends up to it from B (♭7th).

Performance

As these two measures reside entirely within the root position of the F♯ blues scale, standard fingerings apply. Use your ring finger for the bends at the fourth fret, and your index finger for the bends at the second fret.

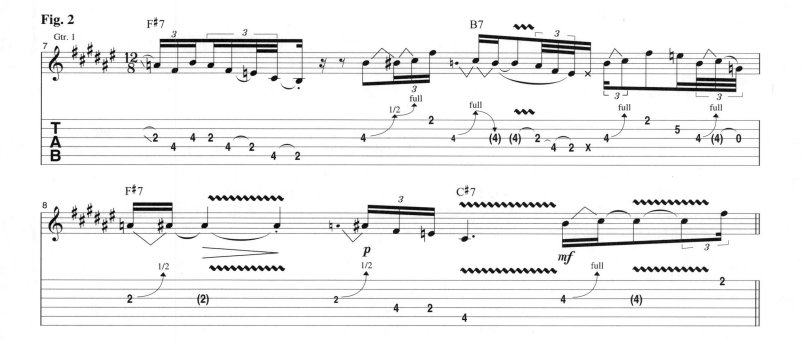

FIGURE 3

Study

Measure 3 (IV chord) of the second eight-bar section of the intro again shows how basic scale tones, skillfully manipulated, can earmark the chord changes. It is particularly illuminating in this instance, where the guitar is only supported harmonically by the bass.

On beat 1, Jimi bends the 2nd (C♯) one half step to the ♭3rd (D), releases the bend and resolves down to the root (B). Over the next two beats he slithers down the F♯ blues scale on the bass strings, crawling on top of the ♭7th (A), ♭3rd (D), interjecting the 2nd (C♯), and resolving to the root (B). On beat 4 he plays the 2nd, 5th (F♯), 6th (G♯), and root notes. He also adds in the double stop C♯/A and the triple stop A, C♯, and F♯ (low to high), which implies a B9 chord—all in all, a lot of tasty information in one measure!

Performance

The half-step bend on the first beat can be pulled down with the index finger. Following a logical fingering of one finger per fret (spanning four frets), the middle finger should be used to engage the half-step bend of C to C♯ in beat 2. This way you can quickly switch to your index finger to repeat the bend from B.

The double and triple stops can be handled by the index finger.

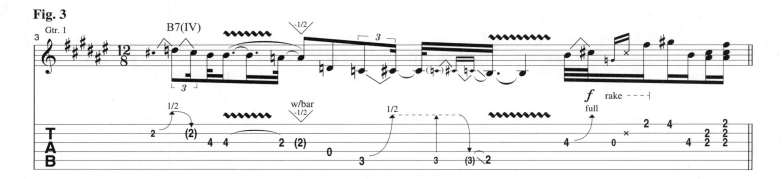

FIGURE 4

Study

Measure 6 of the same section combines double stops in 3rds and 4ths in a seesaw fashion that creates tension and release against the C#7 (V) chord.

After bending the C#/A (root/♭6th) to D/B (♭9th/♭7th), Jimi plays a double-stop run that includes: B/F# (♭7th/4th), A/E (♭6th/♭3rd), E/C (♭3rd/7th), E/B (♭3rd/♭7th), D/A (♭9th/♭6th), F#/C#(4th/root), and F/C (major 3rd/major 7th). Notice the strong blues tones (♭3rd, 4th, and ♭7th), the melodic diatonic tones (major 3rd, 5th, and major 7th), as well as the hip, altered tones (♭6th and ♭9th).

The full bend of E (♭3rd) to F# (4th) and the half-step bend of C (major 7th) to C# (root), ending on the ♭7th (B) brings the F# blues scale back into play.

Performance

The double-stop bend (of unequal pitches) could be played with the middle finger on the G string and ring finger on the B. The double stops at the twelfth and fourteenth frets should be covered by the index finger, the ones at the sixteenth fret by the ring finger, and the one at the fifteenth fret by the middle finger. The oddball E/C in beat 2 (frets 15 and 14) should be played with the middle finger on the A string and the index finger on the D.

The B-string bend at the seventeenth fret can be accomplished with the pinkie (backed up by the ring, middle, and index fingers), while the G-string bend can be reached by the ring finger (backed up by the two fingers behind it).

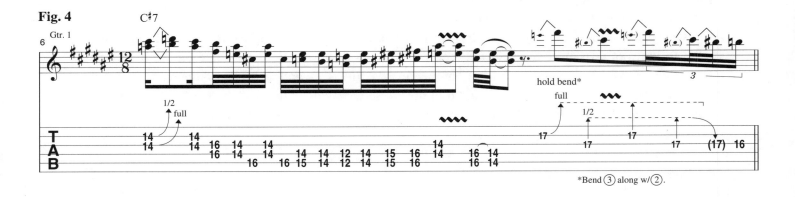

FIGURE 5

Study

The third measure of the verse and its pickup contain a "too cool" vocal/guitar unison line as well as B7 chordal fragments that add melody and extend the harmony.

Jimi plays the unison line in the same octave as his voice. Be sure to notice how he picks more notes than he sings, embellishing both during and after his vocal declaration. The effect, like so much of what he played during his career, is one of simultaneous, independent parts, and a full ensemble sound squeezed out of a trio!

Performance

Standard blues scale fingerings will suffice for the unison line. You should form the chordal shapes with the middle, index, and ring fingers (low to high). By the way, the unmentioned "wolf whistle" that precedes the chordal section should be glissed up with the index finger and down with the ring finger. Like Albert Collins before him, Jimi often tossed off glisses like this to imply spoken words, such as "thank you" at the end of live performances.

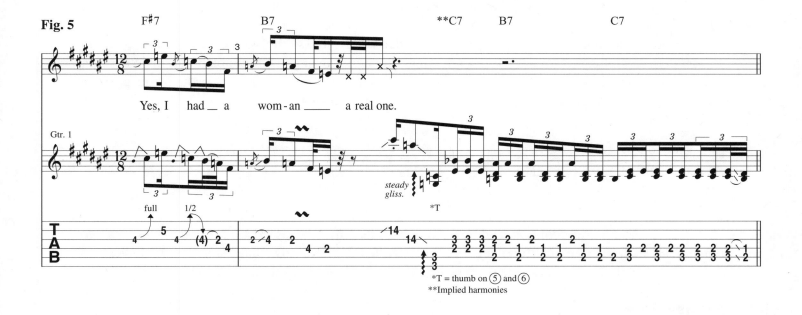

Come On (Part 1)
(Electric Ladyland)

Though taken at a gallop instead of a trot, Jimi's version of Earl King's 1960 R&B hit is quite faithful to the spirit, if not the letter, of the original. Jimi adds a two-measure intro and an ascending chord bridge in the solo. You should know going in that this is not a standard blues, but an R&B tune. It has nine-measure, stop-time verses and twelve-measure choruses.

Earl King did a blues session with master jazzman Barney Kessel in New Orleans, in the fifties. In that session, Kessel gave him a lesson in implying 7th chord voicings with minimal harmonic content. King took the information and incorporated it into "Come On." Shown below are the lower position double stops that he used to imply the I7, IV7, and V7 chord changes.

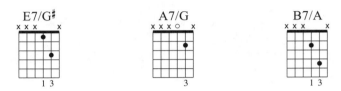

You will notice how cool it is (and how sweet it is) that these forms exist on consecutive frets. Two generations of R&B, soul, and funk guitarists have feasted on these exceedingly hip chordal indicators. Figure 2 deals with King's moveable shapes—which Jimi employed to gainful ends in his version.

FIGURE 1

Study

The two-measure intro moves down the E minor harmonized scale, implying movement from the i to the V7, then resolving to the I chord at the verse. In keeping with the chordal approach in Earl King's original version, Jimi uses double stops for the chords before segueing into the classic intro lick.

Performance

Use your index finger on string 1 and your middle finger on string 2 in measure 1. In measure 2, replace your middle finger with your ring finger.

The "giddy-up" strum corralled by Jimi for the double stops implies an urgency that adds drama to the stop-time that follows.

Fig. 1

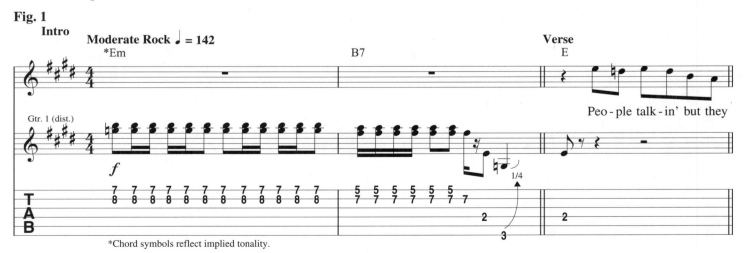

*Chord symbols reflect implied tonality.

FIGURE 2

Study

As he did with the intro, Jimi announces right off that he is going to put his stamp on the hooky chorus. In the first measure, he emphatically hammers on to B from A, where King had matter-of-factly started his run with the B on the downbeat.

In the second and fourth measures, Jimi extends King's original dominant 7th harmony to a 7#9 triple stop for the I chord. Likewise, at the end of the second measure, he boosts the IV chord to a 13th triple stop. In the third measure (IV chord), Jimi plays a Mixolydian mode bass run that implies an A dominant tonality.

The fifth measure contains a series of pull-offs derived from the E blues scale to complement the I chord. Measure 6 returns to the IV chord, and Jimi responds with a C#/G (3rd/b7th) double stop, implying A7, like the one King played in his version. The difference is that Jimi places his chordal forms between the fifth and eighth frets, rather than around the first and open positions like Earl King. Below are the double- and triple-stop shapes used by Jimi.

Performance

Approach this example like you are playing two guitar parts at once—chords in one measure, and fills in the next, in a typical blues "call and response" manner.

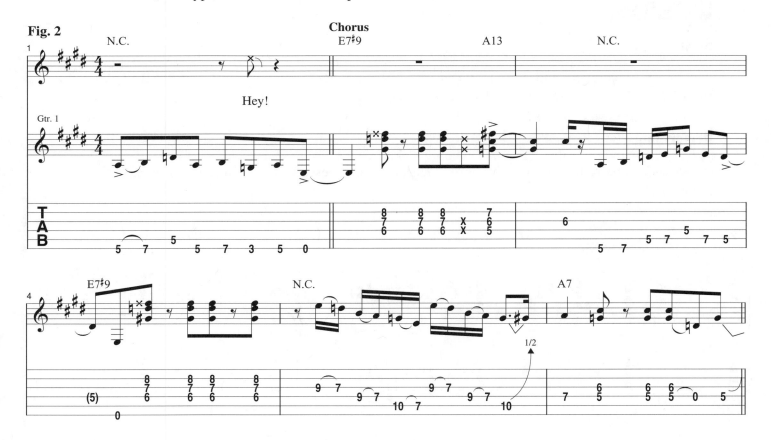

FIGURE 3

Study

Though he adds the root bass note for the B (V) chord in Figure 3, the double stops on strings 4 and 3 are analogous to those used by Earl King. Listen to King's original on *Trick Bag, The Best of Earl King* (1986), and you will hear him incorporate the following chords for the IV and V changes:

Note that Jimi inserts the B♭7 as a passing chord between the V and IV chords.

Performance

You could play the bass notes on string 6 with your thumb (cool!) or your index finger (button-down collar).

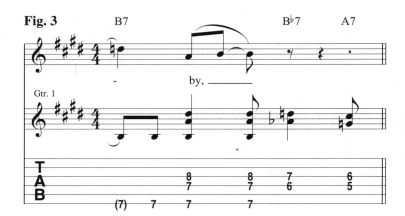

FIGURE 4

Study

Listen up children, and dig how uncle Jimi walks up chromatically from F♯ to B♭ (II to ♭V) and from B9 to D♯9 (V9 to VII9) as a runway into his solo.

Performance

Standard barre chord and 9th chord fingerings are necessary for the successful engagement of Figure 4.

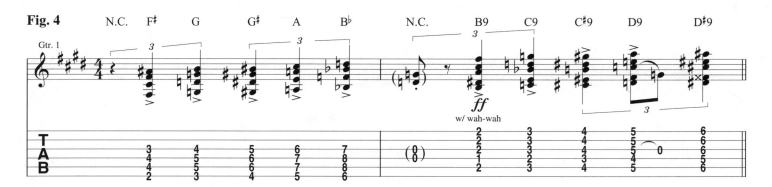

FIGURE 5

Study

Jimi gets downright tasty with his note selection in Figure 5, even as he scalps you from the eyebrows back, with his incendiary, wah-fueled tone.

Over the B (V) chord in the first twelve-measure solo, Jimi plays the F♯ (5th) and C♯ (9th) before bending C♯ to D♯ (3rd) and taking it out with a neat 3rd to sus4 (E) bend.

With the IV chord (A), he comes in hitting the G (♭7th), F♯ (6th), E (5th) and D (4th). Jimi then plays the country bluesman's favorite "train whistle"—the 5th (E) followed by the bent 3rd (C♯). The A (root) is then pulled off to G (♭7th) in preparation for resolution to the E in measure 11 of the solo.

Performance

Over the V chord, bend the C♯ up to D♯ with your ring finger. Over the IV chord, bend the B up to C♯ with your middle finger. Violà!

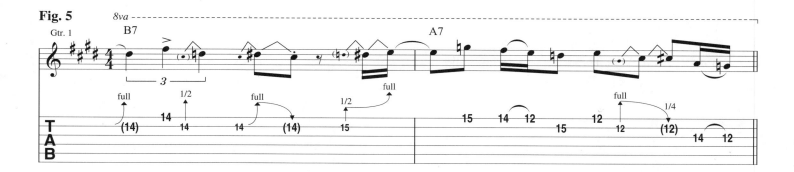

FIGURE 6

Study

In measure 12 of the third chorus, Jimi recycles a lick from Earl King's trick bag. Using the root (E), ♭3rd (G), and 5th (B) in combinations of double stops and single notes, a one-measure modal phrase is concocted that works equally well over the I, IV, or V chord.

Performance

Use the standard fingerings for the root position blues scale.

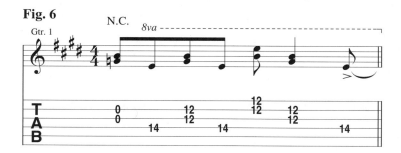

Jam 292
(:Blues)

This instrumental studio jam from 1969 is culled from a period of time when Jimi was playing with friends on a regular basis. Frustrated with the restrictions he was feeling within the Experience, he would stretch like crazy on freewheeling blues jams at every opportunity.

The main theme (Part B) for "Jelly 292" is similar to ones in "Easy Blues" and "Nine to the Universe," from the album of the same name. The second theme (Part D) is derived from the 1940s urban blues classic, "After Hours."

By the way, the sonic evidence on this piece suggests that Jimi jilted his beloved Strat in favor of a Gibson SG Custom, with humbucking pickups.

FIGURE 1

Study

The I chord statement for the chordal "head" consists of Badd9, B♭add 9, and Aadd9 chords, with the root (B) on the low E string. The "add9" chord made frequent guest appearances in Jimi's song catalog. "Hey Joe" and "The Wind Cries Mary" are two such tunes that feature this bit of diatonic harmony.

Performance

The heart of this chord form is a major triad. Play it with your ring finger on the D string, your middle finger on the G string and your index finger on the B string. It is then easy to "add the 9th" on the high E string with your pinkie. Fret the low B note with your thumb.

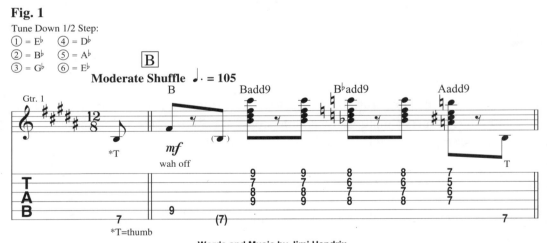

Fig. 1
Tune Down 1/2 Step:
① = E♭ ④ = D♭
② = B♭ ⑤ = A♭
③ = G♭ ⑥ = E♭

FIGURE 2

Study

The IV chord increment for Part B contains E, E♭, and D second inversion (with the 5th on the bottom) major triads.

Performance

A partial barre with your index finger will handle all three chords. Play the E note on string 5 with your index finger.

Fig. 2

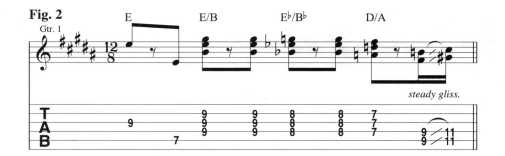

FIGURE 3

Study

Being the creative genius that he was, Jimi comes up with yet another way to play the V (F#) and IV (E) chord changes in measures 9 and 10 of Part B. Theoretically, it is basic and elemental, but his phrasing and attitude breathe life into an otherwise predictable sequence.

After pinning the root in measure 9, Jimi slides up to A#, the 3rd of F#, followed by a C#/F# (5th/root) double stop. He then plays the same relative notes for the F chord, and some musical shorthand (with open strings) for the E chord.

In measure 10, he slides up to the G#, the 3rd of E, before arpeggiating an E major triad in a graceful ascending and descending fashion. The Eb chord is handled like the F# and F chords before, as is the D chord (but played as a full triad rather than a double stop).

Performance

For each chord change in measure 9, slide up to the 3rd with your ring finger and flatten the double stop with your index finger.

For measure 10, use the same fingering combination. Try picking with downstrokes for beat 1 of the E triad and upstrokes for beat 2.

Fig. 3

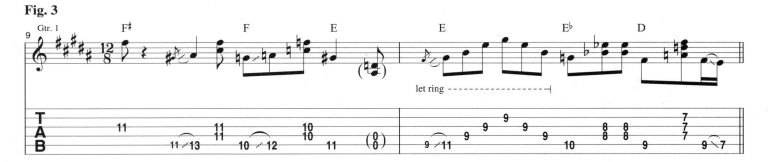

FIGURE 4

Study

As Jimi cruises into Part C, he forges a variation on the chordal pattern of Part B. After establishing the root (B) on beat 1 of each measure, he plays D (IIIb) and C# (II) triads, followed by an E6 (VI) triple-stop which acts as a springboard back to the I (B) chord in the following measure.

Making each chord major creates a powerful set of harmonies. According to diatonic theory, the I (B) chord should be minor, along with the II (C#) chord. In this way the D would function as the relative major chord of Bm. However, this is the "blooze" (read folk music), and blues people can play anything they damn well please, and make it work!

Note that Jimi uses a similar pattern for the IV (E) chord change, with alternative voicings for the triads on the IIIb and II chords being the difference.

Performance

Use standard barre chord fingerings for the D and C♯ chords. Barre the E6 with your ring finger to set your hand in place for the B triad/hammer-on lick that follows in the next measure.

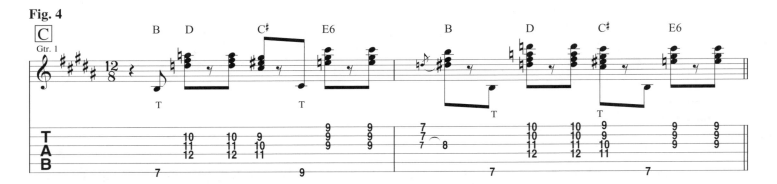

Fig. 4

FIGURE 5

Study

Jimi pulls a slick double-stop trick for the V-to-IV change in measures 9 and 10 of Part C. Phrasing with triplets, he plays A/F♯ (♯9/root) for the V chord. He then moves up the neck two frets (in contrary motion to the direction of the bass line), where the double stop becomes B/G♯ (5th/3rd) over the IV (E) chord.

For your information—if the chord change between these two measures was I-to-IV, the same double stops could be included. In that case the A/F♯ would function as the ♭7th and 5th of B! Check out Chuck Berry's "No Particular Place to Go" to hear this move in action.

Performance

You could use either the middle and index fingers, or the ring and middle fingers, to access the double stops. (Note: Parts D and E contain the bass line that serves as the second, main theme of "Jelly 292.")

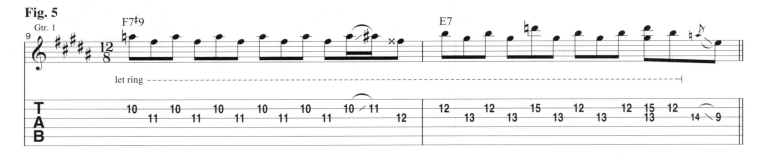

Fig. 5

FIGURE 6

Study and Performance

The second chorus (Part G) of Jimi's solo is a terrific lesson in continuity, intensity, and logic. Let us examine it in its entirety, measure by measure.

Measure 1 (I chord): Jimi steps in with that most traditional of blues guitar licks—the root (B) on string 1 followed by the ♭7th (A) on string 2, bent up a full step to the root and vibratoed. He then repeats a similar lick but bends up a half step (to A♯, the major 7th) before clanging all the way up to B. (Use standard fingerings.)

Measure 2 (I chord): Sustaining the bent root, Jimi adds vibrato, then releases and pulls off down to the 5th (F♯). With the 5th being a somewhat neutral tone, neither implying resolution nor any leading-tone motion, Jimi is free to begin a new but related idea. Sliding up to the 4th (E), he rolls across the 5th and root, and bends the ♭3rd, on string 1, up a full step to the 4th. He then repeats the bend, again sustaining it across the bar line. (Use standard fingerings.)

Measure 3 (I chord): As Jimi starts to close in on the chord change to the IV (E), he turns the wick up on his improvisation. Crossing into measure 3, he wrenches the ♭3rd up one and one half steps to F (♭5th). He then holds the musical tension by repeating the bend twice more before ratcheting down one half step to E (4th). Staying within the blues box, Jimi plays a snappy run containing the root (B), 5th (F♯), ♭3rd (D), and ♭7th (A). (Use standard fingerings.)

Measure 4 (I chord): Gearing up for his big push to the IV chord, Jimi repeats the last phrase from the previous measure. On beats 3 and 4, he bends the E up to F♯ (5th), followed by the F♯ bent up to G♯ (6th). He then sustains the G♯ across the barline where it functions as the major 3rd, or target note, of E (IV). (Bend the E and F♯ notes with your ring finger.)

Measure 5 (IV chord): After releasing the G♯ (3rd) down to F♯ (9th), Jimi shifts positions and locks his hand into the root position of the E blues scale at the twelfth fret. He does a quick resolution to the root (E) followed by a half-step bend on the B string of the ♭7th (D) to the major 7th (D♯), segued directly into a full-step bend to the root.

In a move derived more from rural blues than urban blues, he sustains and vibratos the ♭3rd (G) for two beats. This bluesy dissonance sets up the more melodic sequence in measure 6. (Use standard fingerings.)

Measure 6 (IV chord): Jimi slides into the "happy" major 3rd (G♯), followed by the 5th (B), root (E), and 9th (F♯) bent up a full step to G♯ and then one and one half steps to A (4th). Another bend of F♯ to G♯ solidifies the IV chord tonality before he hammers and pulls the root and 9th, ending on the ♭7th (D). (Use standard fingerings.)

Measure 7 (I chord): Staying in the "Albert King box" (directly above the root position), Jimi works the 4th (E) and 5th (F♯) before landing hard on the 3rd (D♯) and vibratoing. He then glisses into the 5th in the root position blues box, followed by the resolution to the root (B) and two springy bends—the 3rd (D♯) pushed up to the F (another cool ♭5th, as seen previously in the third measure) and a full step to the 4th (E).

Measure 8 (I chord): Jimi pushes the full step bend a *little* harder now, achieving a 1 1/4 step microtone for one beat. This *slightly* sharp note (like what Buddy Guy wrings out of his ax on a regular basis) makes for a dynamic contrast with the melodic 5ths, 6ths, and 9ths that follow. On beat 4, he plays his trump card by bending the ♭7th (A) up *two* full steps to the 9th. (Use standard fingerings, bending the A note with your ring finger.)

Measure 9 (V chord): Sustaining the C♯ across the bar line (where it becomes the stable 5th of F♯), Jimi releases to the A (♭3rd) and bends up one half step to the major 3rd (A♯). Staying within the blues box, he enumerates the root (F♯), 7th (E), 4th (B) and ♭3rd (A) before resolving to the root. (Use standard fingerings.)

Measure 10 (IV chord): Picking up momentum even as the progression winds down, Jimi hops back up to the "A.K. box" once again, where he nails the 5th (B), ♭7th (D), and root (E) notes. He then glides seamlessly into the root position blues box of E, playing a traditional T-Bone Walker-style lick consisting of the major 3rd (G♯), 5th, root and ♭7th, ending with a half-step bend from the ♭7th (D) to the major 7th (D♯). This tantalizing, non-blues bend then resolves to…

Measure 11 (I chord): …the root (B), followed by the ♭3rd punched up one and one half steps to the ♭5th (F), a full step to the 4th (E), released back to the ♭7th and resolved to the root. (Use standard fingerings.)

Measure 12 (I chord): Staying firmly planted between frets 12 and 15 on the B string, Jimi works the D (♭3rd) up to F (♭5th) in a bold display of bluesy delirium, *finally* resolving to the root at the end of the measure. (Use your pinkie, backed up by the ring, middle, and index fingers, to bend the D note. This allows your index finger to easily access the root).

Fig. 6

*Played behind the beat.

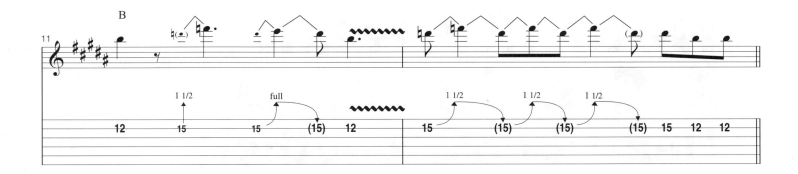

FIGURE 7

Study

The first two measures (I chord) of Part J could be considered the emotional peak of Jimi's long, hard-fought solo. The concept is quite simple, actually. For the better part of two measures, he bends the ♭7th (A) at the seventeenth fret up a whole step to the root (B) and sustains and vibratoes it like a demon. He then bends to the root again. The articulation and sheer logic of this section, after several choruses of wicked riffing, makes for a memorable, satisfying, and compelling blues statement.

Performance

Use the ring finger, backed by the middle and index (natch!), to execute the single string-bends. The double-string bend in measure 2 can be accomplished by catching the E and B strings under your ring finger, backed up by the middle and index. Push the E into the B, bending both together. The fact that the E has to travel to meet the B automatically raises its pitch first. Therefore, when you bend the B up one half step, the E is bent approximately one whole step, due to the distance between the strings.

Be aware that starting with Part K, Jimi bookends his solo with themes similar to Parts C and D. His penchant for controlling the chaos in his music by imposing a compositional framework is brilliant.

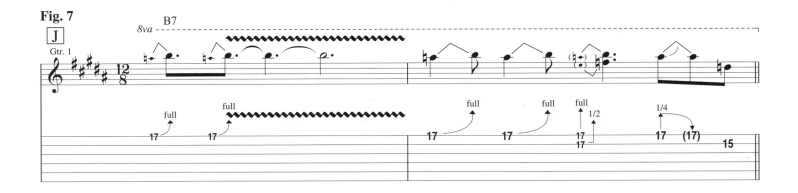

Hear My Train A Comin' (Get My Heart Back Together)

(Acoustic version from :Blues)

For those who saw the 1973 Warner Brothers documentary, "Jimi Hendrix" (released on video in 1984), one amazing scene stood out—there sat Jimi, on a wooden stoop in a photographer's studio, wrapped around an acoustic 12-string (1960 Zamaitis), performing a haunting, riveting solo acoustic version of "Hear My Train A' Comin'." Jimi seemed to be making a conscious, if not calculated, attempt to delve into the roots of his being. Revealing influences as diverse as Tommy Johnson, Skip James, Lightnin' Hopkins, and John Lee Hooker, he turned London, 1967 into Mississippi, 1927.

This rendition has a loose, spontaneous quality, helped out in large part by the unequal length of each section: After an unusual eight-measure intro (IV–V–I–I, I–IV–I–V), verse one is eleven measures (I–I–I–I, I–I–I, V–IV–I–V); verse two is ten measures (I–I–I–I, I–I, V–IV–I–I) and is followed by an eight measure solo based around the I chord; and the last verse is twelve measures in length (I–I–I–I, I–I–I–I, I–I–IV–I), with a strange two-measure diminshed turnaround tacked on as a short, rubato coda. Even for an unaccompanied solo piece, the time is fluid and in a constant state of expansion and contraction.

This is a challenging tune from a man known for technically daunting material. It will translate well onto a six-string acoustic or electric guitar, but be cognizant that Jimi is tuned down *two* whole steps. I do not recommend doing this unless you use extremely heavy gauge strings—.012 to .056, at least. What would probably be better is to stay at concert pitch (A 440) and use the recording to help with the phrasing, but learn the licks off the transcription (key of E).

FIGURE 1

Study

The first two measures of the unorthodox intro show the inner workings of a voracious musical mind. Jazz musicians refer to this as having "big ears." In other words, Jimi could hear advanced concepts, such as hip chord substitutions, even if he could not explain them theoretically.

See that Jimi plays C♯ (3rd), B (9th), and G (♭7th) to infer an A dominant chord in measure 1. In measure 2, though, the real cool stuff happens. The inferred D major (♭VII chord of E) could also be seen as an implied, altered V (B) chord! Remember, a ♭VII chord (usually dominant, sometimes minor or major) can substitute for the V. Here is the way it works: The D/F♯ *could* be read as the root and 3rd of D, or it *could* be the ♯9th and 5th of B. The half-step bend sharps the 5th. Dig it!

Performance

Pull off from your ring finger to your index, ending up with your middle finger on the G note. In measure 2, place your pinkie on the D and your index finger on the F♯.

Fig. 1

Tune Down 2 Steps:
① = C   ④ = B♭
② = G   ⑤ = F
③ = E♭ ⑥ = C

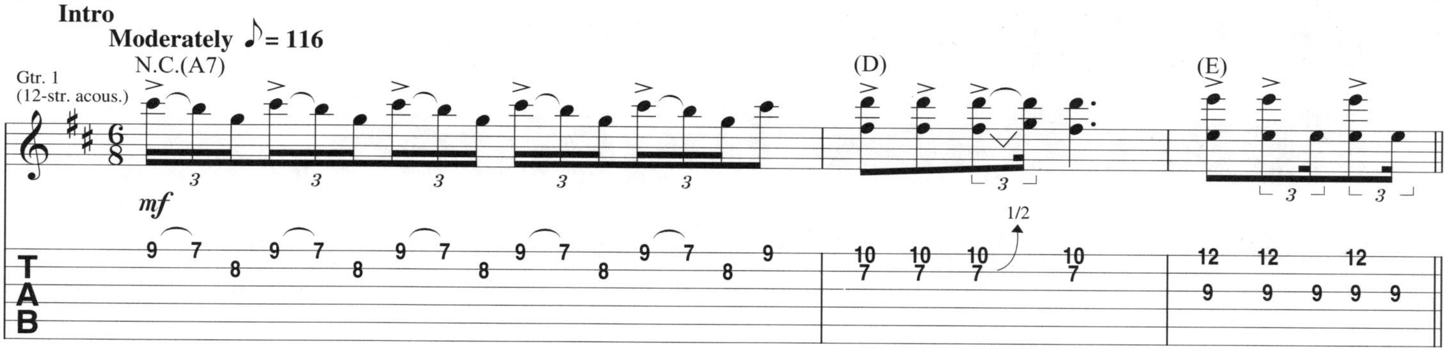

Intro
Moderately ♪ = 116

Gtr. 1
(12-str. acous.)

N.C.(A7)   (D)   (E)

FIGURE 2

Study

As he does so well, Jimi mimics his vocal line with the "voice" of his guitar in the first measure of the verse. To be sure, we are not talking about an aria here, but the effect is mesmerizing nonetheless. Corking out of the open string position of the E blues scale, Jimi plays (and sings, in unison) the ♭3rd, root, and ♭7th (G, E, D) notes. He accurately follows every syllable of his vocal line, adding a pull-off on beat 3 as an embellishment. As a structural device, he brackets the measure with root (E) notes played on the open, low E string.

Performance

Play all fretted notes with the ring finger.

Fig. 2
Verse
Slow Blues ♩ = 66
N.C. (E7)

wait a - round   the   train ___   sta - tion.

Gtr. 1

FIGURE 2

Study

In measure 6 of the first verse, Jimi plays a fill reminiscent of his original intro to "Hey Joe." After establishing his tonality with the open E strings and a hammer-on from the 4th (A) to the 5th (B), followed by a common "E blues" triple stop (A, D, and E, low to high), he plays a familiar descending pattern on beats 3 and 4. Starting with the open high E string, Jimi plays the E note at the fifth fret, on the B string, in unison. After plucking the open high E again, he then plays the D at the third fret on the B string, paired with the open high E. A pull-off to the 4th (A) from the 5th (B) is followed by the open G and B strings, and resolution is made to the trilled E (root) note on the D string at the second fret.

The implied chord change is E7, but this sequence gives the *impression* of harmonic, as well as melodic, movement from E to E7sus4 to E7.

Performance

Hammer from the 4th to the 5th with your index and ring fingers. Catch the fretted notes of the triple stop with your index and middle fingers. This will enable you to easily shift your position up to fret 5 for the descending "Hey Joe" pattern. If you use your index finger to play the fretted E and D notes, your hand will be back in a perfect position to play the slide from the 5th to the 4th with your middle finger.

I recommend executing the trill with your strong middle finger.

FIGURE 4

Study

In measure 5 of the second verse, Jimi plays a partial turnaround pattern that performs the same function as Figure 3—an instrumental bridge between the I (E) chord and V (B) chord.

He begins it in a similar fashion, as well. After nailing down the E chord change with a variety of open and fretted root notes (and the hammer/slide from the 4th to the 5th), Jimi plays 6ths and a triple stop that suggest E°7 and E♭°7, resolving to the hammered major 3rd (G♯).

Performance

Play the 6ths with your middle finger on the G string and your ring finger on the high E string. Hammer on to the G♯ note with your index finger.

FIGURE 5

Study

Measures 1 and 2 of the solo have Jimi scat-singing while accompanying with the guitar in unison an octave lower. Staying in this lower register, on the bass strings, presents a powerful contrast to the guitar figures that precede it. Part of the allure is the rich bass sonorities emanating from the handmade, 1960 Tony Zemaitis 12-string, tuned down two full steps. Jimi's svelte, unforced vocals glide effortlessly over this substantial foundation.

Performance

The ring and index fingers should be used through measure 1 of the solo. Use your middle finger for the notes on the second fret in measure two.

FIGURE 6

Study

After teasing us with bits and pieces of the traditional "Robert Johnson diminished turnaround," Jimi finally gives it up at the finale. Notice his personal embellishment of the quick Esus4.

Performance

Play the double stops with your middle and ring fingers. Play the triple stops with your middle, index, and ring fingers (low to high). Finger the E5 chord in the standard "folk guitar" fashion, then play the Bb (b5th) note on the G string with your pinkie, shifting it down to the A note (sus4) before pulling it off to your index finger for the G# (3rd).

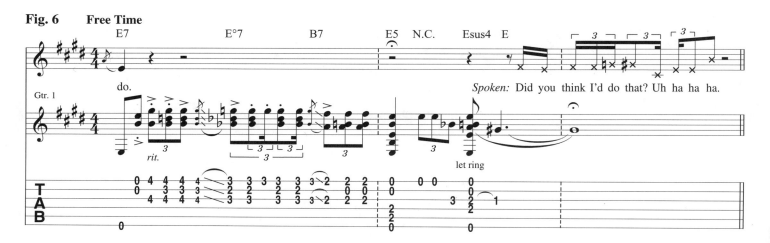

Hear My Train A Comin' (Get My Heart Back Together)
(:Woodstock)

This volatile electric version of the Hendrix blues classic was the first one to be captured on tape. Jimi had been playing and developing it on tour with the Experience, and by the time of Woodstock, he was ready to give it full production values. Backing him up were Mitch Mitchell (drums), Billy Cox (bass), Larry Lee (guitar), and two percussionists, Juma Sultan and Jerry Velez. Known collectively as the Gypsy Sun & Rainbows Band, they were actually a performing version of what Jimi had been calling the Electric Church, or Sky Church. Various other participants also included Buddy Miles (drums), Noel Redding (bass), and Lee Michaels (Hammond organ). Jimi was anxious to expand beyond the trio format and to feel like more of a member, rather than the sole focus of a musical group. And, even though he *is* the show on this recording (as well as most of the Woodstock performance), the larger rhythm section encouraged him to go wider and deeper with his improvisations.

FIGURE 1

Study

After Jimi's rubato (free time) intro, he breaks into the electric "Hear My Train A' Comin'" theme. This primal blues lick, formed around the root (E), 4th (A), and ♭3rd (G), is played at the twelfth fret in the octave position of the E blues box. On beat 4, as a pickup into the next modal measure, Jimi plays a snappy hammer/pull combination with the ♭7th (D) and root notes to lead back to the open, low E string.

The vamped "blues in E" has a history that probably dates back into the nineteenth century. Certainly Jimi's take on this classic American songform has a long pedigree. The two "modern" exemplars of this subgenre are Lightnin' Hopkins and, to a lesser extent, John Lee Hooker. Without question, Jimi was influenced by both in his "Hear My Train A' Comin'" and "Voodoo Chile."

Performance

Use standard blues scale fingerings.

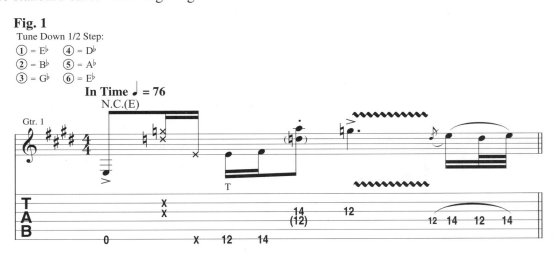

Fig. 1

Tune Down 1/2 Step:
①= E♭ ④= D♭
②= B♭ ⑤= A♭
③= G♭ ⑥= E♭

In Time ♩ = 76

FIGURE 2

Study

Jimi alters the phrase slightly by substituting the G (♭3rd) in the bass figure on beat 2, and more significantly, by fattening up the main part on beat 3 with double stops. In addition, he trills between the root and ♭7th notes on beat 4.

The double stops C♯/A (6th/4th) and B/G (5th/♭3rd) are a staple of minor key blues as practiced by the late Magic Sam, as well as by Otis Rush and Buddy Guy on the West Side of Chicago in the late 1950s and early 1960s. In this context, they operate in that ambiguous major/minor netherworld that is a part of the blues.

Performance

Use standard blues scale fingerings.

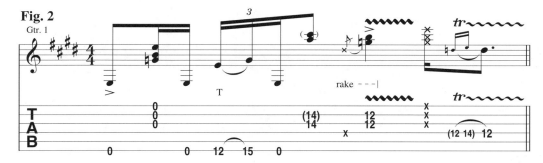

FIGURE 3

Study

When Jimi brings in the whole band, he deepens and darkens his double-stop tonality. Ending on the G/D (♭3rd/♭7th) on beat 3 produces a haunting harmony, befitting his vocal lament to follow.

He also changes his pickup notes on beat 4. By bending the ♭3rd (G) up a quarter step and resolving to the root, he ties it into "Catfish Blues," the Muddy Waters connection, and his own "Voodoo Chile."

Performance

Hoist up the ♭3rd, at the fifteenth fret, with your pinkie.

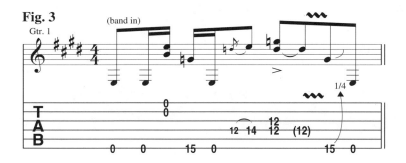

FIGURE 4

Study

Blues guitarists had been banging away in the root position pentatonic box for almost 100 years by the time Jimi started performing, yet he still managed to be creative within this protean scale.

Dig the E5 dyad that precedes the bend of the 4th (A) to the 5th on beat 2. Jimi then blends in the ♭7th on the fifteenth fret of the B string, repeats the bend, and follows it all with the ♭3rd, (G) bent one half step to the major 3rd, before resolving to the root.

Performance

Play the B/E double stop with your middle and index fingers. This will facilitate bending the G string with your ring finger. Play the ♭7th (D) that follows the G string bend with your pinkie. Bend the ♭3rd on beat 4 by pulling (towards the floor) with your index finger.

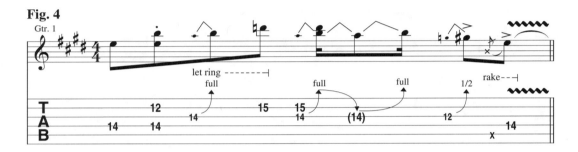

FIGURE 5

Study

Jimi gets way down "beneath the underdog" with this fifth variation on a blues theme. After hammering from the open ♭7th (D) to the root (E) at the second fret, he slides up from G♯/B (3rd/5th) to B/D (5th/♭7th) and then down to A/C♯ (4th/6th). The implied chordal movement (in 6ths) is E/B, E7/D and F♯m/C♯, a combination of diatonic and blues harmony. Note that this is a slightly more sophisticated way of playing a harmonized boogie bass line that would imply E5, E7, and E6, if played on strings 6 and 5.

Now, Jimi is properly ready to sing about his baby!

Performance

Use your middle and index fingers for the E and E7 shapes, shifting to your ring and index fingers for the F♯m.

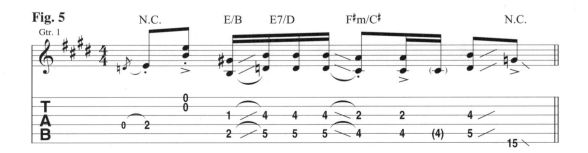

FIGURE 6

Study

Jimi's dramatic release from the simmering tension of his modal verse consists of inferred D (♭VII), G (♭III), and A (IV) chords. In order to heighten the sense of propulsive forward motion in this section, he harmonizes each change into a boogie bass line. The D change he plays in the open position while barring for the G and A.

Performance

By anchoring your index finger on the G string at the second fret, you will easily be able to reach the other notes in the D chord change with your middle, ring, and index fingers. The G and A boogie patterns should be barred with your index finger at the third and fifth frets, respectively.

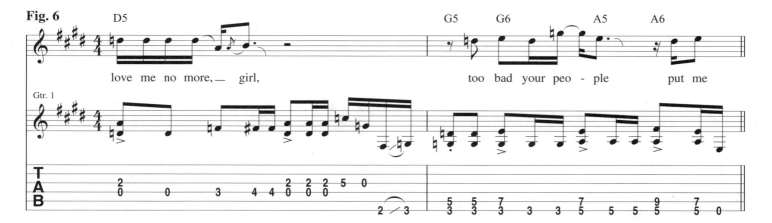

FIGURE 7

Study

As in "Catfish Blues" and "Voodoo Chile," Jimi sings and plays a quick chorus in unison. It is a simple line, with the guitar in exact sync and in the same octave, using the open position E blues scale.

Performance

Bend with your ring finger, and play the D♯ with the same digit. Play the vibratoed E at the fifth fret with your pinkie (if you dare!)

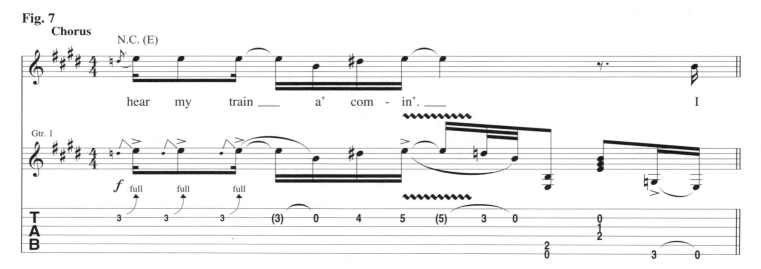

47

FIGURE 8

Study

The last variation on the "Hear My Train A' Comin'" theme is in the open, root position of the E blues scale. After trilling on the root at the second fret D string, Jimi bends the D (♭7th) note on the B string up a full step to the root, releases it and vibratoes the D. He then plays a full step bend, pushing A (4th) up to B (5th) on the G string, followed by the clever technique of raising the open G a full step by pressing down on the string *behind* the nut! It is a refreshing effect after all the caterwauling that Jimi did in the previous section with the wah, Univibe, whammy bar, and distortion.

Performance

Trill with your middle finger. Bend the D note with your ring finger, and pull *down* on the A note (string 3) with your middle finger, backed up by the index finger. Then reach behind the nut and push down on the G string with your index finger.

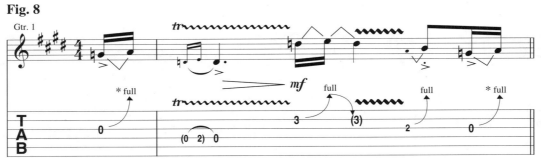

Fig. 8

*Open-string bends articulated by pushing down on string behind nut.

Red House
(Smash Hits)

This is the flagship of the Hendrix blues fleet. Recorded in 1966, Jimi wanted it to be on his first American album, *Are You Experienced?* (1967), but he was overruled by the "suits" and had to settle for it appearing on the English offering instead. Through his lobbying efforts, it was included on *Smash Hits* (1969) from whence it has become a veritable blues anthem. Players as diverse as John Lee Hooker and country picker Junior Brown have recorded stunning versions.

Though "Red House" would turn into an epic blues opus in concert, this succinct studio track is a masterpiece of fills, phrasing, tone, drama, and attitude!

FIGURE 1

Study

Robert Johnson contributed this chordal move to the lexicon of the blues in the thirties. Muddy Waters, among many others, also employed it to great effect as an intro, or as the first three measures of a twelve-bar blues. But, where these illustrious gentlemen used the B°7 chord shape to imply a dominant IV chord change (F, A♭, and D *could* be read as E7♭9), Jimi uses it literally, to imply a B°7. Ironically, Noel Redding plays a B♭ bass note underneath, implying in *his* mind a move from B7 to B♭7! (He could have just pedalled on the B bass note and had the desired diminished tonality. Billy Cox, where were you when Jimi needed you?)

Performance

Set your hands thusly for the two measures: middle finger on the G string, index finger on the B string, and ring finger on the high E string.

Fig. 1
Intro

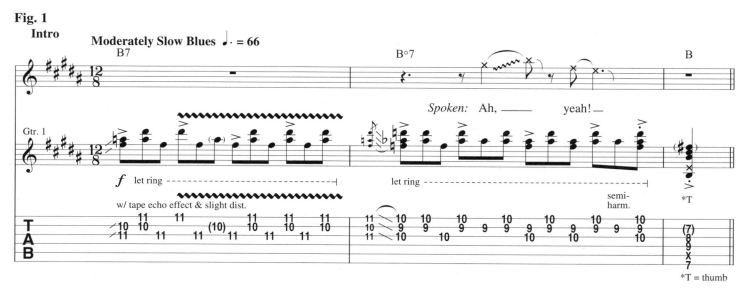

FIGURE 2

Study

In measure 1 of the verse, Jimi plays one of his patented double-stop/hammer-on licks that relates to the I (B) chord and the IV (E) chord coming up. On beat 4, he hammers the G# (6th) while outlining B/F# (root/5th) to imply a melodious B6 chord.

If we looked at this phrase as anticipating the IV chord, the hammered double stop implies the 3rd and 5th chord tones of E. The descending pattern then becomes, relative to E, the 5th, 9th and 5th. This concept of anticipating the next chord change with kicks or fills was a key ingredient in the pioneering improvisational styles of Django Reinhardt and B.B. King.

Performance

Barre the top two strings at the seventh fret with your index finger. Maintain the barre as you upstroke through the B, F#, and B notes.

FIGURE 3

Study

In measure 5 of the verse, Jimi plays the same lick as in Figure 2, only this time it *is* over the IV (E) chord. As previously mentioned, his intuitive sense of composition, especially regarding motifs and themes, informs his work with a certain deep-seated order and structure.

Performance

Use the same fingerings as in Figure 2.

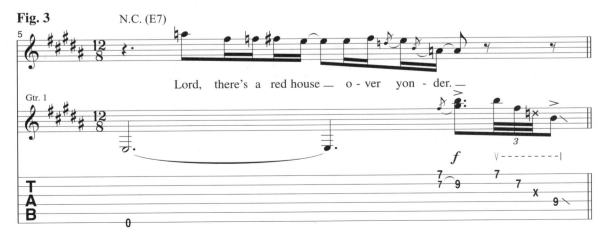

FIGURE 4

Study

Jimi derives drama from a moody bass fill that gracefully connects the V (F♯) chord to the IV (E) chord in measures 9 and 10 of the verse.

Over the V chord he plays a run containing the root (F♯), 2nd (G♯), 4th (B), 5th (C♯), and ♭7th (E) from the F♯ Mixolydian mode. He ends the phrase on beat 1 of the IV chord with the root (E) played on the low E string.

Performance

Use your index and ring fingers for the fretted notes.

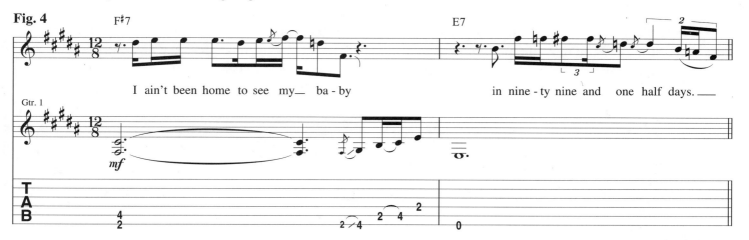

FIGURE 5

Study

In measures 5 and 6 (IV chord) of the second verse, Jimi again spins a dramatic-sounding lick that delineates the E tonality. Starting with the open E (root) string on beats 1 and 3, he slides up from the F♯ (2nd) to the G♯ (3rd) and then down from the root to the ♭7th (D). He quickly follows this with the open low E string as a whole note in measure 6.

The stark simplicity of this sequence epitomizes blues theory in its effectiveness as a chordal indicator.

Performance

Use your index and ring fingers for the fretted notes.

FIGURE 6

Study

Oh "Music, sweet music," to steal a quote from "Manic Depression." The sliding 6ths in measures 9 and 10 of the second verse are heartbreaking in their lyrical beauty.

Popularized by T-Bone Walker and Johnny Moore in the forties, these harmonized double stops can say more with less, when it comes to indicating chord changes. Over the F♯ (V), Jimi slides between C♯/E (5th/♭7th) and D♯/F♯ (6th/root). For the E (IV) chord (but starting on beat 4 of the V chord), he plays B/D (5th/♭7th) and C♯/E (6th/root)—the same notes, now with a different meaning.

Performance

Use your middle and ring fingers on the G and E strings, respectively. Pick the strings only once for the first double stop, sliding back and forth for the rest. You could do this by strumming across the top three strings as you mute the B string with your middle finger. Or, you could pluck the G string with the pick while simultaneously plucking the high E string with your middle finger.

This section of "Red House" is one of the gems, from a number bursting with musical treasures.

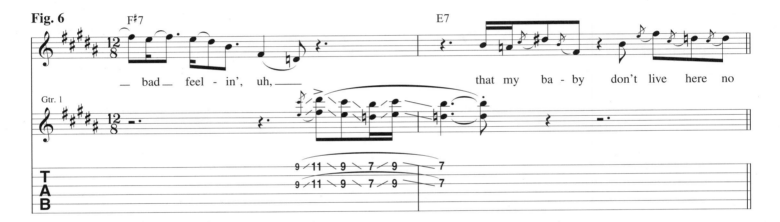

FIGURE 7

Study

In measures 1 and 2 of the third verse, Jimi employs the sliding 6ths to indicate the movement of the I (B) to the IV (E) chord. He hits F♯/A (5th/♭7th), slides up to G♯/B (6th/root), then follows with the root note as an embellishment before sliding back down.

In measure 2 (IV chord) he plays the same 6ths as in Figure 6.

Performance

Because the B note is inserted between the sliding 6ths in measure 1, a different fingering must be used. Barre across strings 4, 3, and 2 with your index finger and pluck the appropriate notes with your pick and middle fingers. After sliding up to the ninth fret, reach up to the twelfth fret with your pinkie for the octave root note. Simultaneously pick the double stop at the ninth fret again, and slide down to fret 7. Use the same fingering and plucking technique for measure 2.

Fig. 7

*Played ahead of the beat.

FIGURE 8

Study

Jimi's turnaround pattern in measures 11 and 12 of the third verse flows beautifully through the implied I–IV–I changes.

On beats 1 and 2 of measure 11 (I chord), Jimi elucidates on the F♯ (5th), B (root), and C♯ (9th) notes. On beats 3 and 4 (IV chord) he plays the G♯ (3rd), B (5th), and D♯ (7th) notes.

On beat 1 of measure 12 (I chord) he repeats the bend to D♯ (3rd) to nail the B tonality. He then resolves the tune with a ♭II (C7) to I (B7) chord change.

Performance

Use standard blues scale fingerings in measure 11. In measure 12, play the triple-stop dominant chords like you were fingering an open position D major chord.

Give a listen to Freddie King's original studio recording of "Have You Ever Loved a Woman" to hear a similar end turnaround.

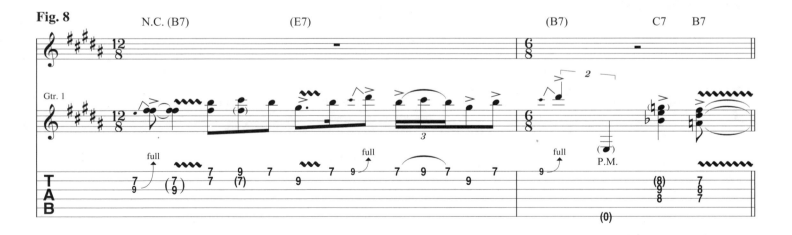

Fig. 8

Red House

(:Woodstock)

With his legendary Woodstock performance following close upon the commercial success of *Smash Hits,* Jimi was able to treat the crowd to a galvanizing presentation of a familiar recording.

It is worth knowing that bassist Billy Cox *pedals* on the root (B) as Jimi does his B7 to B°7 triple-stop move in measures 1 and 2 of the intro. However, in measure 2 of the second twelve-bar section of the intro (Figure 1), Cox *does* make the change with his bassline to the IV (E) chord, thank you very much!

FIGURE 1

Study

Jimi sounds like he is going to repeat measures 1 and 2 of the intro, but halfway through measure 2 (IV chord) he glides up the neck with sliding 6ths, resolving at the fourteenth fret (F♯/A, the 5th/♭7th of B) at the start of measure 3. The A/C at the seventeenth fret functions as a "grace" double stop, down to G♯/B at the sixteenth fret, which functions as the 3rd and 5th of E, implying an E major chord. The G/B♭ at the fifteenth fret implies an E°7 chord (like you would find in a blues turnaround).

Performance

Use your middle and ring fingers on the G and E strings.

Fig. 1

Tune Down 1/2 Step:
① = E♭ ④ = D♭
② = B♭ ⑤ = A♭
③ = G♭ ⑥ = E♭

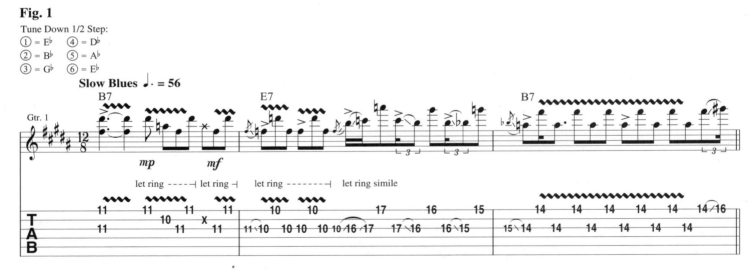

FIGURE 2

Study

In measure 4 (I chord) of the first verse, Jimi plays a series of chromatic pull-off licks on the high E, B, and G strings. Contained within this "box" are the notes from the previous sliding 6ths (G♯/B, G/B♭, and F♯/A) plus the 3rd (D♯), ♭3rd (D,) and 2nd (C♯) notes on the B string. In other words, *beaucoup* major scale and blues scale harmony to go over the I (B) chord change.

As Jimi goes "outside" the standard blues tradition, he presents a welcome break from the potential predictability of the "gapped" pentatonic (or blues) scale.

Performance

Render these cascading sixteenth-note triplets by setting your index, middle, and ring fingers in place on each string, and then striking the note at the sixteenth fret and pulling off to the fifteenth and fourteenth frets.

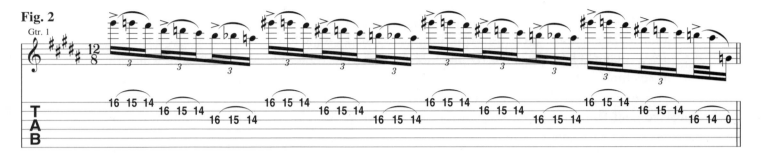

FIGURE 3

Study

Measure 3 (I chord) of the second verse has several spicy double-stop variations that add musical tension over the B chord before resolving in measure 4.

Jimi starts by bending the 4th (E) on the G string a full step to the 5th (F♯) while maintaining the ♭7th (A) note on the B string. As he holds down the A, he drops to the ♭3rd (D), goes back to the 4th (E), then bends the 4th up a half step to F (♭5th) before completing the cycle by bending the 4th up to the 5th in measure 4!

Performance

Keep your pinkie on the A note, using your ring finger (backed up by the middle and index) for the bends. Play the D note with your index finger.

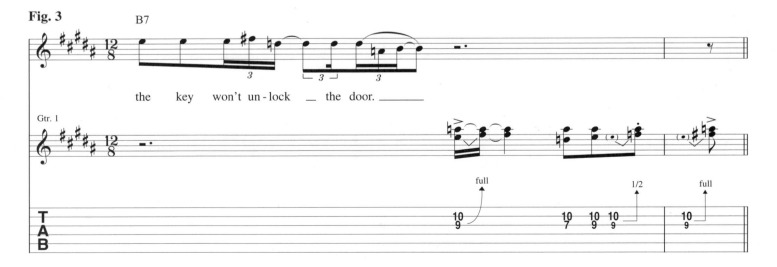

FIGURE 4

Study

In measures 3, 4, and 5 of the fourth verse, Jimi plays a chordal accompaniment with dominant forms. In other live performances of "Red House"—most notably the ones from Albert Hall (1969) and Winterland (1968)—he explored this concept in even greater depth.

Rhythm guitar playing was as important to Jimi Hendrix as every other aspect of his music. Even in situations like this one, where he had a (barely audible) second guitarist, it is *his* rhythm that *always* drives the band.

Starting in measure 3 (I chord) he implies B7 and C13 chords with double and triple stops. In measure 4 (I chord) he repeats the B7 and C13 (an "organic" grace chord) until beat 3, where he starts a chromatic climb up the neck from B9, resolving to E7 in measure 5 (IV chord).

Notice the variety of voicings and rhythms that Jimi uses during these two measures of B (I chord). Never content to be just a passive strummer, he invests his rhythm parts with all the dynamics and passion of his lead playing.

Performance

For the B7 and C13 chords, set your fingers like this: index on string 6, middle on string 4, ring on string 3, and pinkie (when needed) on string 2.

For the B9 through D♯9 chords, do it this way: middle finger on string 6, index on string 4, ring on string 3, and pinkie on string 2. The E7 chord can be played like the 9th chords, but move your middle finger to string 5.

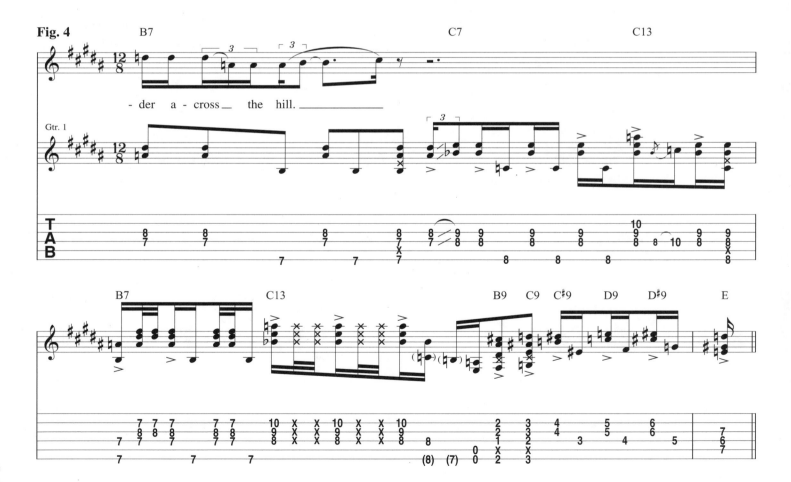

Gypsy Eyes
(Electric Ladyland)

Though much more R&B and funk, than blues, "Gypsy Eyes" is built from the ground up on twisted blues licks. It is a compositionally creative piece with three main sections:

1) An intro/bridge, based on a modal blues scale phrase;

2) A chorus where the guitars play in unison and in harmony with Jimi's vocal; and

3) Verses constructed around a bass pattern that outlines ♭III, IV, and I chord changes.

FIGURE 1

Study

The intro/bridge lick is a one-measure pattern based on the A blues scale. It leans heavily on the root (A) and ♭7th (G) notes, with the E/C (5th/♭3rd) double stop accenting the phrase with a chordal stab.

The example in Figure 1 is taken from measure 2 following the first chorus.

Performance

Use standard blues scale fingerings for this section. By pulling down on the double stop with your index finger, you should be able to raise the C (♭3rd) note on the G string one quarter step for the desired "slurry" effect.

Fast alternate picking is required for the requisite funk feel on the bass notes.

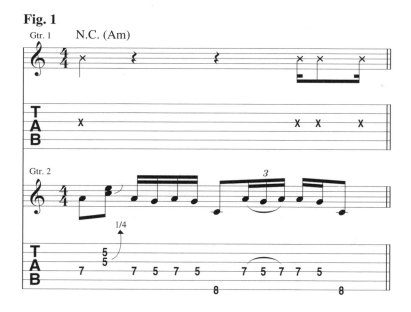

Fig. 1

FIGURE 2

Study

The last three measures of the chorus, where Jimi repeats "I love you, gypsy eyes," contain a delectable twin guitar part in sync with his vocal.

Guitar 1 tracks Jimi's vocal in unison, in the same octave, using the root, ♭3rd, 5th, and ♭7th (A, C, E, and G) notes. Guitar 2 plays the same thing, but one octave lower.

Performance

Use standard blues scale fingerings for both parts.

Fig. 2

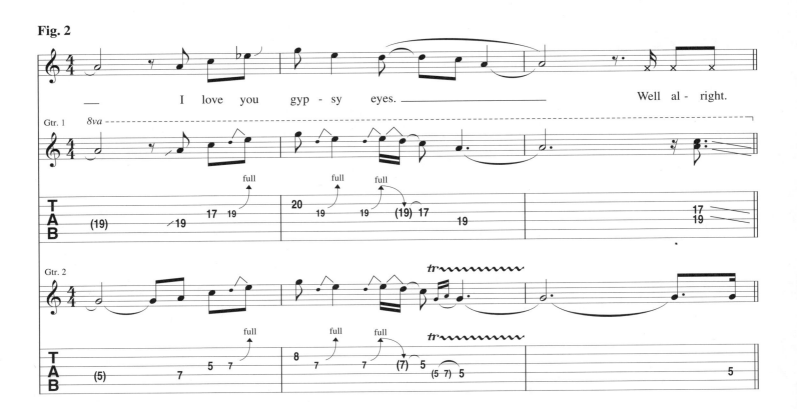

FIGURE 3

Study

Measures 1, 3, and 5 of the verse have a double-stop phrase that echoes the harmony and sounds prevalent throughout "Gypsy Eyes." The simplicity of the concept is utterly brilliant; Jimi utilizes 3rds (E/C and F#/D) along with judicious bends and the root (A) note to help imply C (♭III), D (IV), and A (I) chords.

Performance

Play the E/C with your index finger and the F#/D with your ring finger. The bend on beat 3 can be achieved by pulling down with your ring finger, which *should* result in the unequal intervals.

Fig. 3

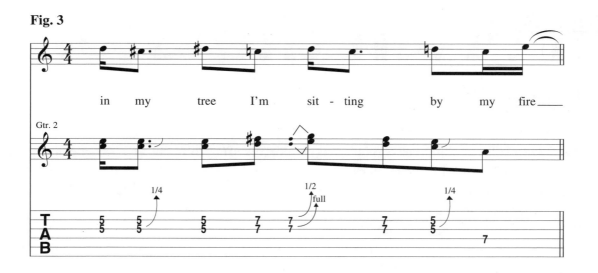

in my   tree   I'm   sit - ting   by   my   fire____

In From the Storm

(Cry of Love)

As one of the last studio tracks completed (but not mixed) by Jimi before his tragic death, "In From the Storm" shows how far his Delta blues had progressed. Like "Gypsy Eyes," it's composed of several related themes, with rhythmic and time changes, but it still has the "call and response" feel of a modal country blues throughout the main verses.

By the way, an illuminating comparison can be made between "In From the Storm" and Jeff Beck's "Rice Pudding" (from *Beck-Ola,* 1969). It is well known, of course, that Jimi was a big fan of Beck and had expressed particular admiration for "Beck's Bolero"—dare we be so bold as to suggest that Jimi's monumental version of "All Along the Watchtower" was significantly influenced by Beck's homage to the Spanish dance?

FIGURE 1

Study

The theme for the verse is an unpretentious minor pentatonic pattern that briefly and simply implies an F#m7 chord change by emphasizing the ♭7th (E), root (F#), and ♭3rd (A) notes.

Performance

Use standard blues scale fingerings, performing the microtonal bend on the A (♭3rd) note, on beat 3, by pulling down with your pinkie.

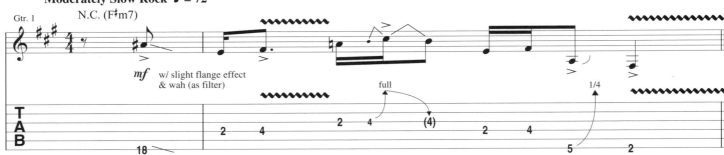

Fig. 1

Intro

Moderately Slow Rock ♩ = 72

FIGURE 2

Study

Highlighting the "call and response" dynamics of the verse, Jimi plays a basic octave figure (Gtr. 1) to infer the E chord change.

Performance

Place your index finger on string 5 and your ring finger on string 3. Either mute string 4 (D) with your index finger as you strum down across the strings with your pick, or hold the pick firmly between your thumb and index finger only, and pick string 5 while simultaneously plucking up on string 3 with your right hand middle finger. Jimi would often play licks like this, as well as other fingerstyle figures, by burying the pick in the palm of his left hand while plucking with his thumb and index finger.

Fig. 2

Verse

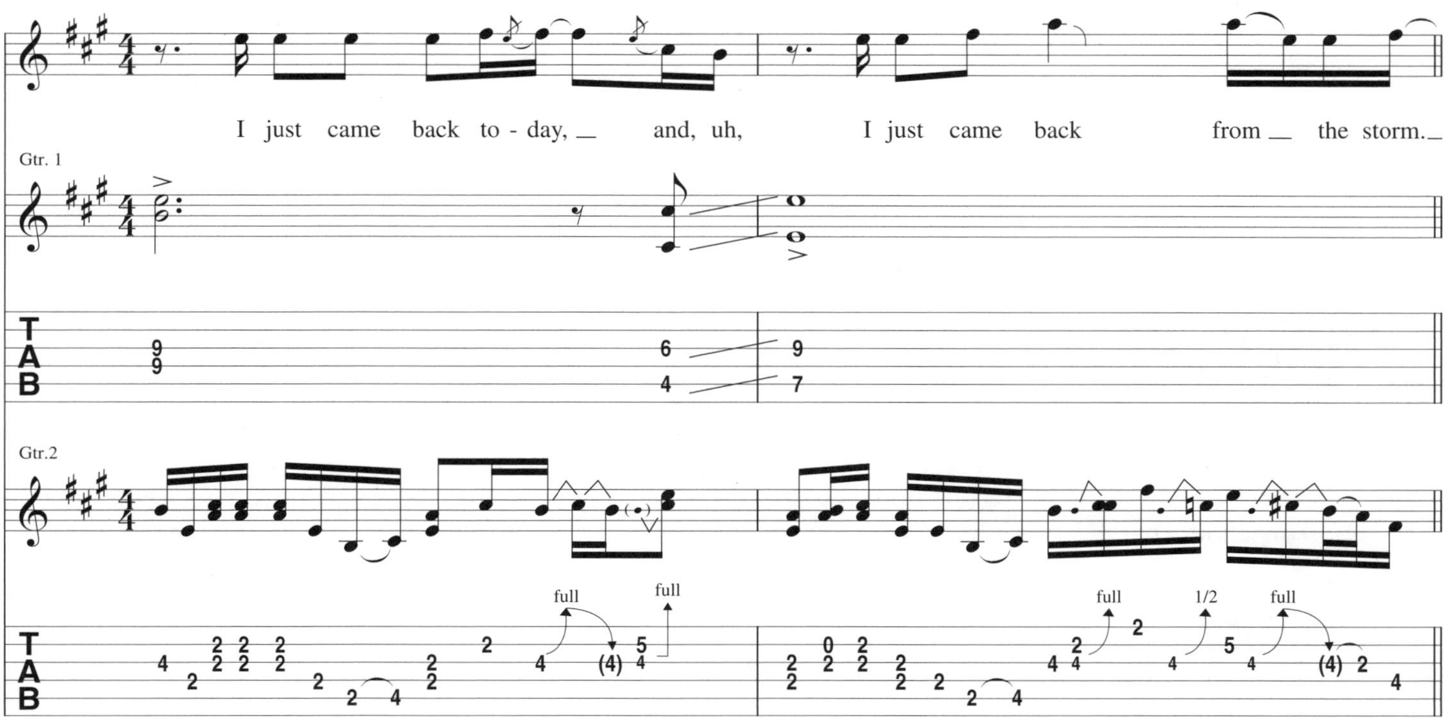
E
I just came back to - day, __ and, uh, I just came back from __ the storm. __
Gtr. 1
Gtr.2
full
full
full
1/2
full

FIGURE 3

Study

With Gtr. 2, Jimi reveals his understanding of the subtleties inherent within even the most basic chord forms. After arpeggiating and then strumming the C♯7♯9 chord, he plays an octave E (with an added 5th) and an implied Esus4. (The sus 4th, A, is the major 3rd of F, the next chord.) He then infers the F with an octave (with an added 5th) before playing the ♭5th (C), 4th (B), and root (F♯) of the F♯ blues scale as a pickup phrase to connect back to the F♯m7 chord change in the next measure.

Performance

Low to high, play the chord forms as such: C♯7♯9 with middle, index, ring, and pinkie; E5 with index, ring, and pinkie; Esus4 with index and pinkie; F5 with index, ring, and pinkie.

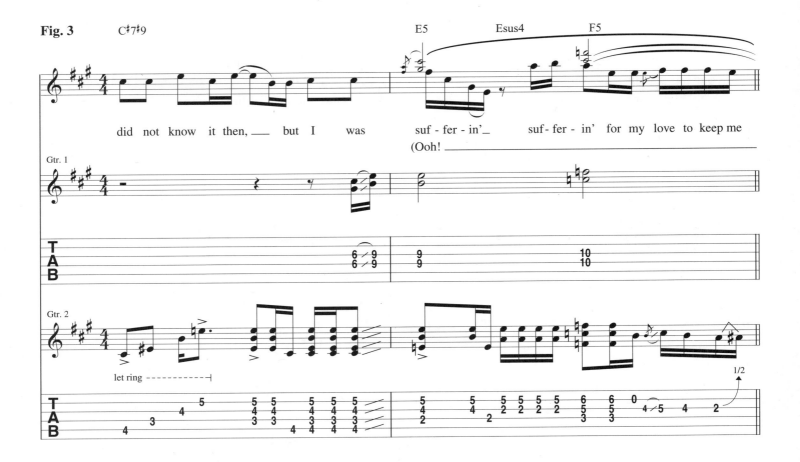

Fig. 3

FIGURE 4

Study

The five-measure interlude that follows the bridge again displays Jimi's chordal diversity. In Gtr. 2, he plays a broken C# octave (with added 5th) and a cool C#7#9 chord with open strings, plus a standard fretted C#7#9, ending up back on that open C#7#9 voicing.

In measure 4, Gtr. 1 plays an octave E (with added 5th) against an open-string version of the C#7#9 chord (minus the root, with the major 3rd on the bottom). Note that E and B notes from the octave E lick are contained within the C#7#9 chord (as the #9th and ♭7th notes). You should also know that an E major triad (G#, B, and E) would also go nicely over top of the C#7#9 chord, inasmuch as the G# (3rd of E) could function as the 5th of the C#7#9 chord. The relationship between E major and C#7#9 is similar to that of relative major and minor chords. Though the C#7#9 chord is technically a dominant chord, the #9th (E) imparts a minor quality to this ambiguous sonority (#9th=♭3rd).

Performance

The most logical fingerings for these voicings should be self-evident by this point in your study!

Fig. 4

Interlude

A Tempo ♩ = 80

Guitar Notation Legend

Guitar Music can be notated three different ways: on a *musical staff*, in *tablature*, and in *rhythm slashes*.

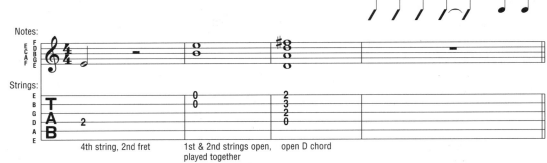

RHYTHM SLASHES are written above the staff. Strum chords in the rhythm indicated. Use the chord diagrams found at the top of the first page of the transcription for the appropriate chord voicings. Round noteheads indicate single notes.

THE MUSICAL STAFF shows pitches and rhythms and is divided by bar lines into measures. Pitches are named after the first seven letters of the alphabet.

TABLATURE graphically represents the guitar fingerboard. Each horizontal line represents a string, and each number represents a fret.

4th string, 2nd fret   1st & 2nd strings open, played together   open D chord

HALF-STEP BEND: Strike the note and bend up 1/2 step.

WHOLE-STEP BEND: Strike the note and bend up one step.

GRACE NOTE BEND: Strike the note and bend up as indicated. The first note does not take up any time.

SLIGHT (MICROTONE) BEND: Strike the note and bend up 1/4 step.

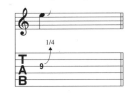

BEND AND RELEASE: Strike the note and bend up as indicated, then release back to the original note. Only the first note is struck.

PRE-BEND: Bend the note as indicated, then strike it.

VIBRATO: The string is vibrated by rapidly bending and releasing the note with the fretting hand.

WIDE VIBRATO: The pitch is varied to a greater degree by vibrating with the fretting hand.

HAMMER-ON: Strike the first (lower) note with one finger, then sound the higher note (on the same string) with another finger by fretting it without picking.

PULL-OFF: Place both fingers on the notes to be sounded. Strike the first note and without picking, pull the finger off to sound the second (lower) note.

LEGATO SLIDE: Strike the first note and then slide the same fret-hand finger up or down to the second note. The second note is not struck.

SHIFT SLIDE: Same as legato slide, except the second note is struck.

TRILL: Very rapidly alternate between the notes indicated by continuously hammering on and pulling off.

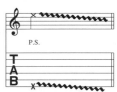

TAPPING: Hammer ("tap") the fret indicated with the pick-hand index or middle finger and pull off to the note fretted by the fret hand.

NATURAL HARMONIC: Strike the note while the fret-hand lightly touches the string directly over the fret indicated.

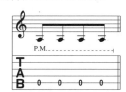

PINCH HARMONIC: The note is fretted normally and a harmonic is produced by adding the edge of the thumb or the tip of the index finger of the pick hand to the normal pick attack.

PICK SCRAPE: The edge of the pick is rubbed down (or up) the string, producing a scratchy sound.

MUFFLED STRINGS: A percussive sound is produced by laying the fret hand across the string(s) without depressing, and striking them with the pick hand.

PALM MUTING: The note is partially muted by the pick hand lightly touching the string(s) just before the bridge.

RAKE: Drag the pick across the strings indicated with a single motion.

TREMOLO PICKING: The note is picked as rapidly and continuously as possible.

VIBRATO BAR DIVE AND RETURN: The pitch of the note or chord is dropped a specified number of steps (in rhythm) then returned to the original pitch.

VIBRATO BAR SCOOP: Depress the bar just before striking the note, then quickly release the bar.

VIBRATO BAR DIP: Strike the note and then immediately drop a specified number of steps, then release back to the original pitch.